Introduction to Property Law in India

By Siva Prasad Bose and Joy Bose

Published by Joy Bose

Copyright © 2022 Siva Prasad Bose and Joy Bose

All rights reserved. No part of this book may be reproduced in any form or by an electronic or mechanical means, including information storage and retrieval systems, without permission in writing from the publisher.

Contents

Dedication

Preface

Chapter 1: What is property law

Chapter 2: Types of Property

Chapter 3: Possession and Ownership

Chapter 4: History of Property Law

Chapter 5: Transfer of Property Act 1882

Chapter 6: Law Related to Sale of Immoveable Property

Chapter 7: Law Related to Mortgage of Property

Chapter 8: Law Related to Lease of Property

Chapter 9: Law Related to Exchange of Property

Chapter 10: Laws Related to Gift of Property

Chapter 11: Indian Succession Act 1925

Chapter 12: Sale of Goods Act 1930

Chapter 13: Law on Easements

Chapter 14: Laws Related to Cooperative Housing Societies

Chapter 15: Real Estate (Regulation and Development) Act, 2016 – RERA

Chapter 16: Land Acquisition Laws in India

Chapter 17: Benami Transactions and Benami Property Law

Chapter 18: Partition and Joint Ownership of Property

Chapter 19: Property Taxation and Municipal Duties

Chapter 20: Property Disputes and Court Remedies

Chapter 21: Conclusion

Glossary of Legal Terms

About the Authors

Other Books by Siva Prasad Bose

Dedication

This book is dedicated to all the people in India who own property, or thinking of owning property or are fighting property cases in Indian courts. It is hoped that knowledge of property law will be of benefit to them.

Preface

Property law encompasses a wide spectrum of legal principles governing the ownership, transfer, management, and protection of property. In a country like India, where property often represents both a basic necessity and the single largest investment for most families, a clear understanding of these laws is essential, not just for legal professionals, but for every citizen.

This book aims to serve as an accessible and practical guide to the foundational aspects of property law in India. We introduce readers to the historical evolution of property law, from ancient traditions and philosophical influences to the emergence of modern statutes and digital reforms. The book focuses particularly on immovable property, such as land and buildings, but also touches upon other forms of property and their unique legal treatment.

Key legislations, such as the Transfer of Property Act 1882, the Indian Succession Act 1925, and related acts, are explained in clear and straightforward terms. Recent developments, including the Real Estate (Regulation and Development) Act (RERA) and the digitalization of land records, are also covered to help readers understand the contemporary landscape.

Whether you are planning to buy, sell, inherit, or invest in property, or if you are involved in property disputes or wish to avoid common pitfalls, this book provides an essential starting point. It is our hope that this work will empower readers to navigate property transactions and legal processes with greater confidence, awareness, and peace of mind.

Chapter 1: What is property law

In this chapter, we discuss the concept of property laws in general terms.

The term 'property' in property law includes both tangible and intangible property. Tangible property refers to things that can be touched, including moveable property such as money, gold, electrical appliances, electronic gadgets and furniture, and immoveable property such as land and buildings. Intangible property includes things that cannot necessarily be touched but still have value and come under the definition of property. Examples of intangible property include intellectual property such as patents and trademarks, and financial instruments such as bank accounts and shares in a company.

In this book we will mostly focus on immoveable property such as land. However, the laws are mostly equally applicable for moveable property as well.

1.1 Definition of Property

The term "property" refers to anything that can be owned, controlled, or transferred. Property can be broadly classified into two types:
- Movable property: Property that can be physically moved from one place to another (e.g., furniture, vehicles, jewellery).

- Immovable property: Property that is fixed and cannot be moved (e.g., land, buildings, trees attached to the land).

In legal terms, immovable property is the main focus of property law in India.

1.2 Importance of property law or land law

Since the amount of land in a country like India is limited, and there is limited capacity for expansion of available land for housing, the land law or property law has become more important.

Everyone needs a place to live. Hence, land is a necessity. Property prices are rising faster in recent years, especially in the metro cities in India. Hence for many people buying property such as a flat or villa is their life's biggest investment, in addition to being a place to stay. Many people cannot afford to buy their own property and must stay in rented apartments, whose rents and deposits are also increasing at a rapid pace.

Bank loans for buying land and constructing a flat is usually the way most people fund their property purchase. It is typically the biggest loan people take in their lives and would spend a good few years to repay. Therefore, as an investment decision, buying property is a major decision of one's life.

For those unfortunate enough to be involved in property disputes in the Indian courts, these typically take up years or decades and end up costing a lot of money.

For all the above reasons and more, knowledge of property law and land law are very important. It is critical to have an awareness of the prevailing property laws in India and how they affect us.

1.3 What does property law deal with?

Property law is a branch of civil law that governs the various forms of ownership, possession, transfer, and use of property. In India, property law has evolved through legislation, case law, and customary practices. Understanding property law is important for landowners, tenants, buyers, developers, and legal professionals alike.

Property law deals with the rights and obligations connected with the property people own, rent or have a lease on, as well as the implications of transferring the same to other parties.

It deals with all aspects of the property such as mortgage loans taken from banks, taxes to be paid, registering, gifting and leasing a property, how to prove ownership of the property, how to get property as part of a will, how to pass it to one's heirs, how to rent or give property as rent, how to enable one to access basic amenities such as sunlight and water through a neighbor's land and so on.

1.4 Sources of Property Law in India

The sources of Indian property law include:
- The Constitution of India

- Statutory laws, such as:
  - The Transfer of Property Act, 1882
  - The Indian Easements Act, 1882
  - The Registration Act, 1908
  - The Indian Succession Act, 1925
  - The Hindu Succession Act, 1956
  - The Benami Transactions (Prohibition) Act, 1988
- Judicial precedents or case laws
- Customary practices and religious laws (Hindu and Muslim law)

1.5 Importance of Property Law

Property law plays a vital role in:
- Defining legal ownership
- Regulating transactions involving sale, lease, gift, mortgage, etc.
- Ensuring fair inheritance
- Protecting against encroachment or illegal occupation
- Facilitating registration and transfer of title

Without a legal framework, property disputes would become more frequent and chaotic.

1.6 Key Concepts in Property Law

Some of the fundamental legal concepts in property law include:

- Title: Legal ownership of a property.
- Possession: Physical control or occupation of a property.
- Ownership: The right to use, enjoy, sell, lease, or dispose of property.
- Transfer: Legal process of changing ownership through sale, gift, will, etc.
- Encumbrance: Legal burden such as a mortgage or lien on the property.

1.7 Classifications of Property

Property in Indian law can be classified in various ways:

1. Corporeal and Incorporeal Property:
    - Corporeal: Tangible and visible (land, house).
    - Incorporeal: Intangible rights like easements, copyrights.
2. Real and Personal Property:
    - Real property: Immovable (land and buildings).
    - Personal property: Movable items.
3. Public and Private Property:
    - Public: Owned by the state (roads, parks).

- Private: Owned by individuals or companies.

4. Ancestral and Self-Acquired Property:
   - Ancestral: Inherited from forefathers.
   - Self-acquired: Purchased or acquired by one's own effort.

1.8 How property can be transferred between two parties

There are multiple ways in which property transfer can happen. It can be through either voluntary transfer or involuntary or compulsory transfer. Land may be transferred when both the parties are living or when one has died and the other party gets the property by means of succession.

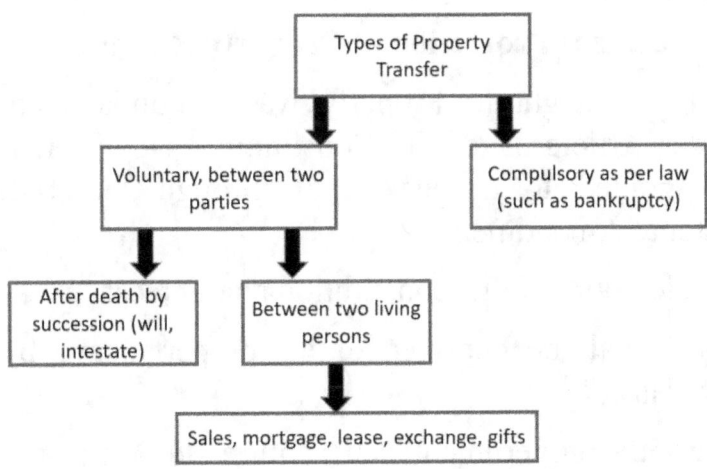

Figure: Illustration of the types of property transfer

Depending on the type of transfer, the relevant Indian laws will apply.

For example, for voluntary transfer of property between two living parties, the applicable law is Transfer of Property Act 1882, which covers sales, mortgages, leases, exchanges and gifts.

For laws related to succession, where property is transferred from a deceased person to a living person, the Indian Succession Act (ISA) 1925 is the applicable law.

For compulsory transfers by government or due to bankruptcy and insolvency clauses, various laws can apply. Sale of Goods Act 1930 applies for sale of moveable property, which may be part of the sale of a house or apartment.

1.9 Constitutional Protection of Property Rights

Originally, the Right to Property was a Fundamental Right under Article 31 of the Constitution. However, it was downgraded to a legal right through the 44th Constitutional Amendment in 1978.

Now, Article 300A of the Constitution guarantees:

"No person shall be deprived of his property save by authority of law."

This means the government can acquire property only through legal and compensatory means.

1.10 Conclusion

Property law in India governs the relationship between people and their rights over tangible and intangible assets. It provides the legal framework for owning, transferring, inheriting, and resolving disputes over property. With growing urbanization and investment in real estate, the significance of property law continues to increase.

Chapter 2: Types of Property

This chapter introduces the different types of property as recognized under Indian law. A clear understanding of these categories is important to determine the legal treatment, transfer rights, and obligations of the owner. In this chapter we discuss the types of property from various angles.

2.1 Movable and Immovable Property

Property can be broadly classified into the following:

- **Movable Property**: Refers to items that can be moved from one place to another, such as vehicles, furniture, jewellery, cash, shares, etc. These are governed under the Sale of Goods Act, 1930.

- **Immovable Property**: Refers to property that cannot be moved, such as land, buildings, houses, trees attached to land, etc. This is governed under the Transfer of Property Act, 1882 and the Registration Act, 1908.

2.2 Tangible and Intangible Property

Another way to classify the types of property as per its nature is as follows:

- **Tangible Property**: Property that has physical form and can be touched (e.g. land, gold, vehicles).

- **Intangible Property**: Property that does not have a physical form but has value (e.g. copyrights, trademarks, patents, goodwill).

2.3 Private and Public Property

Yet another common way in which property is referred to as per the nature of its ownership is as follows:
- **Private Property**: Owned by individuals or private entities. The owner has full rights to use, sell, lease, or transfer it, subject to applicable laws.
- **Public Property**: Owned by the government or public institutions (e.g. roads, public parks, government buildings).

2.4 Real and Personal Property

- **Real Property**: Refers primarily to land and things attached to the land such as buildings, crops, and minerals.
- **Personal Property**: Refers to movable assets which are not fixed to land, such as mobile phones, furniture, or bank accounts.

2.5 Corporeal and Incorporeal Property

This is another way property is categorized in legal theory:

- **Corporeal Property**: Property that is material and perceptible by senses. This includes all tangible assets, whether movable (like a car) or immovable (like a house).

- **Incorporeal Property**: Consists of rights over property that are intangible, such as easements (a right of way), lease rights, or intellectual property.

2.6 Ancestral and Self-Acquired Property

This distinction is especially relevant under Hindu succession laws:

- **Ancestral Property**: Property inherited up to four generations of male lineage. Every coparcener has a birthright in such property.

- **Self-Acquired Property**: Property acquired by an individual through their own effort or income. The owner has full rights over its disposal and it does not automatically pass to heirs unless willed.

2.7 Summary

Understanding the classification of property is essential in determining rights, duties, and laws applicable. These categories help in settling issues of transfer, inheritance, taxation, and legal ownership.

Chapter 3: Possession and Ownership

Possession and ownership are fundamental concepts in property law. Although the terms are sometimes used interchangeably, they have distinct meanings and legal implications. In this chapter we go deeper into the difference between the two.

3.1 What is Possession?

Possession refers to the physical control or occupation of property, either with or without legal title.

- Actual Possession: When a person physically occupies a property (e.g. living in a house).
- Constructive Possession: When a person has legal control or claim, even if not in physical occupation (e.g. giving property on rent).

Possession gives rise to certain legal rights, even in the absence of ownership. For example, a tenant has a right to occupy the premises and can seek protection against unlawful eviction.

3.2 What is Ownership?

Ownership means having full legal rights over property. It includes the rights to:

- Possess
- Use and enjoy

- Transfer or sell
- Lease or rent
- Mortgage or gift
- Exclude others from the property

Ownership gives complete authority over the property, unlike possession which may be temporary or partial.

3.3 Kinds of Ownership

- Sole Ownership: The property is owned by a single individual.
- Joint Ownership: Multiple persons own the property together (see Chapter 17 for more detail).
- Co-ownership: Each co-owner has a defined share, even if not physically demarcated.
- Trust Ownership: Ownership is vested in a trustee on behalf of beneficiaries.

3.4 Legal and Equitable Ownership

- Legal Ownership: Recognized by law and registered under appropriate statutes (e.g. name in the title deed).
- Equitable Ownership: Arises where a person has financial interest or rights due to payments made, even if not in official records.

Example: A person who paid for a house registered in another's name may have an equitable interest.

3.5 Ownership vs Possession

The below table summarizes the difference between ownership and possession.

Feature	Ownership	Possession
Nature	Legal right	Factual state
Transferable	Yes	Only if legally allowed
Duration	Usually permanent	Can be temporary (e.g., tenancy)
Enforcement	Enforced through title and legal action	Enforced through rights of occupier

While ownership gives comprehensive rights, possession can still offer protection under law, especially against unlawful dispossession.

3.6 Adverse Possession

This is a doctrine where a person who possesses land openly, continuously, and hostilely for a certain period (typically 12 years in India), without the consent of the original owner, may acquire legal ownership through limitation laws.

Example: If a person occupies abandoned land for 12 years without challenge, they may claim legal title under adverse possession.

It is a controversial but recognized principle under Indian law and is often invoked in land disputes.

3.7 Conclusion

Possession and ownership are closely related but legally distinct concepts. While ownership is a complete and legally recognized right, possession gives certain protections, especially against unlawful interference. In disputes, courts often examine both aspects before deciding the rightful claimant.

Chapter 4: History of Property Law

Land law and property law have a long history. In this chapter, we study some of the main historical laws surrounding land and property in India and other countries.

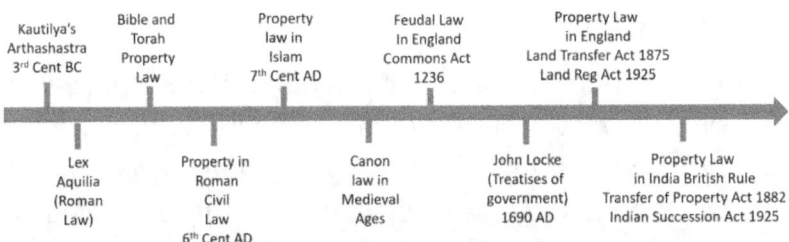

Figure: Evolution of property law in different parts of the world over time

4.1 Property law in Roman times

The Romans had the concept of private property and compensation for wrongful damage to property. They had a law called Lex Aquilia, from 3rd century BC. This law provided for compensation to Roman citizens in case of vandalism and destruction of their property.

One of the provisions of the Lex Aquilia law states "*As regards things other than men and cattle which have been killed, if any one does damage to another, and unlawfully burns, breaks, or ruptures something, let him be ordered to pay its owner whatever that thing is worth in the nearest thirty days."*

4.2 Property law in Kautilya's Arthashastra

Kautilya was a minister in the Mauryan empire of Chandragupta Maurya in India around the 3rd century BC. Kautilya's masterpiece of statecraft, called "Arthashastra" had provisions for land management and division of inheritance.

One of the property related statements in the Arthashastra states "*A father, distributing his property while he his alive, shall make no distinction in dividing it among his sons. Nor shall a father deprive without sufficient reason any of the sons of his share. Father being dead leaving no property, the elder sons shall show favor to the younger ones, if the latter are not of bad character.*"

4.3 Property law in Torah and Bible

As per the original Jewish law described in the Torah, property was only to be inherited and not to be sold to outsiders.

Leviticus 25:23 states "*But the land must not be sold beyond reclaim, for the land is Mine; you are but strangers resident with Me.*"

Later, sale contracts were instituted in Jewish law.

4.4 Property as per Roman Civil Law

As per the Roman civil law instituted by Emperor Justinian in 6th Century AD, land could be owned by individuals and also transferred to others. There was a set procedure to transfer land to others involving witnesses and copper ignots as a mark of the transfer.

4.5 Property law in Islam

Islamic law or shariah law provided for inheritance of property by legal heirs. There was the concept of Waseyya or will, which stated how a person could willingly transfer one third of their property to another upon their death.

The other two thirds would go as per the established rules of the state, as per the concept of Fara'id or Mirath. Fara'id defined how much proportion of the deceased person's property and assets should be distributed to which heirs.

4.6 Property laws in medieval ages

In the medieval ages in Europe, the Canon law of the church largely governed property transactions. It covered things such as wills and property acquisition. It also influenced the law on property in the post reformation era.

4.7 John Locke's views on property rights

Upon the end of feudal era in Europe, philosophers wrote about property rights. John Locke was a British philosopher who wrote about property rights in his book "The Two Treatises of Government (1690)." Locke's theory is called Labor theory of property, where he stated that a person's mixing his labor with the property was what gave him the right to the property. As per Locke, under natural law, all people have the right to "life, liberty, and estate (property)." Locke thus argued for individual property rights as natural rights that could not be denied to anyone.

A number of other European philosophers and intellectuals also upheld the right to private property. 17th century Dutch judge Grotius held that the state has to compensate individuals if they expropriate their property. Utilitarian English philosopher Jeremy Bentham held that property is an expectation created by common practice and law. John Stuart Mill held that individual property rights are associated with liberty and freedom. Hegel held that property is a manifestation of the personality of an individual person, and thus argued for protection of property. Kant had a conception of legal ownership of property as distinguished from physical possession of it, and held the view of private property rights as essential for freedom.

4.8 Property law in England

English property law descended from a combination of Roman law and various feudal laws governing land and other property in England. These included the Commons Act 1236 and Statute of Westminster 1285.

After reformation, important reformed property laws were brought in England including the following:

- Land Transfer Act 1875
- Land Registration Act 1925 which provided for land registration
- Wills Act 1837 that dealt with transfer of property through Wills
- Law of Property Act 1925.

Some of these acts, called Settled Land Acts, increased the power of property to the persons who were settled on it rather than the legal owners, who were often landed aristocrats who charged high rents.

4.9 Property law under British rule in India and later

With the advent of British rule in India and their creation of courts and a legal system modelled on the British legal system, property law changed in India.

The British rulers brought a number of laws in India which were counterparts of similar laws existing in United Kingdom in that time. Based on this, the legal system in India largely became similar to the common law system practiced in UK and USA and other countries, although it did maintain some aspects of traditional systems such as personal laws of various religions.

Introduction to Property Law in India

The three main laws related to property in British India were as follows:

- Transfer of Property Act 1882: This was the main act that stated the rules for transfer of moveable and immoveable property to another person.
- Sale of goods act 1930: This governed sale of property.
- Indian Succession Act 1925: This governed succession of property to heirs or upon making a will

Taken together, the above laws lay the foundation of property law in India. The same laws have survived in independent India with some modifications.

Before independence, most of the land in India, especially agricultural land in villages, was governed under various systems such as zamindari, ryotwari and talukdari systems. The landowners such as Zamindars owned the land and leased it to peasants who cultivated the land and paid the landlord a fixed price or part of the produce as rent for the land. If there was a famine or natural calamity, the peasants still had to pay the rent and the ownership remained with the zamindars. In this sense it was unfair. But gradually some types of reforms were instituted to reduce the burden on peasants and even provide them the option of ownership.

The Constitution of India also provides for the right to property, although it is currently not in the list of fundamental rights which it had been previously. Article

300A of the Indian constitution says "No person shall be deprived of his property save by authority of law."

4.10 Evolution of Property Law in India

Property law in India has evolved over centuries:

- Ancient Hindu and Islamic laws governed property matters within religious communities.
- The British introduced codified laws like the Transfer of Property Act, 1882, Indian Succession Act, etc.
- Post-independence, land reform laws were enacted to abolish zamindari and promote land ceiling, tenancy rights, and redistribution.
- Modern developments like RERA, Benami law, and digital land records have increased transparency.

4.11 Modern International Influences on Property Law

Property law globally has continued to evolve, influenced by international conventions, treaties, and declarations. International agreements like the Universal Declaration of Human Rights (UDHR) and various UN covenants recognize property rights as fundamental to human dignity and economic stability. For example, Article 17 of the UDHR states:

"Everyone has the right to own property alone as well as in association with others. No one shall be arbitrarily deprived of his property."

Such declarations influence national legislations worldwide, including India, emphasizing fair compensation, protection from arbitrary state action, and respect for private ownership.

4.12 Influence of Judicial Decisions and Common Law

Judicial decisions, also known as precedents, play a significant role in shaping property law. This common-law tradition, inherited from English law, means that judgments from higher courts such as the Supreme Court of India or High Courts serve as guidelines for future cases. For instance, landmark cases involving property rights, tenancy, inheritance, and land acquisition have shaped current interpretations and applications of Indian property law.

A notable Indian judgment includes the landmark case of Kesavananda Bharati vs. State of Kerala (1973), which reaffirmed the government's right to acquire property but within limits of fairness and due process, maintaining the basic structure of the Constitution.

4.13 Post-Independence Land Reforms in India

After India's independence, property law underwent significant transformation through land reforms aimed at addressing inequality and feudal exploitation. The goals included:

- Abolishing zamindari systems and intermediaries.
- Establishing ceilings on landholdings.
- Redistribution of surplus land among landless farmers.
- Securing tenancy rights and protection against arbitrary eviction.

Notable legislation includes the Uttar Pradesh Zamindari Abolition and Land Reforms Act (1950), West Bengal Land Reforms Act (1955), and similar state acts that significantly reshaped property ownership in rural India.

4.14 Digitalization and Property Records Modernization

In recent decades, the Indian government has implemented digital initiatives to modernize land records, bringing greater transparency and reducing disputes. Key initiatives include:

- Digital India Land Records Modernization Programme (DILRMP), aiming to digitize property records, establish clear ownership, and simplify land transactions.
- Establishment of state-level online land record portals such as Bhulekh (Uttar Pradesh), Bhoomi (Karnataka), and Banglarbhumi (West Bengal),

which provide easy access to land records, maps, and related data.

These initiatives represent a crucial modern step in the evolution of property law in India, making transactions more transparent and secure.

References

- https://en.wikipedia.org/wiki/Lex_Aquilia
- https://www.wisdomlib.org/hinduism/book/kautilya-arthashastra/d/doc366088.html
- https://en.wikipedia.org/wiki/History_of_English_land_law
- https://www.islamicwillsusa.com/property-distribution-islam/
- https://en.wikipedia.org/wiki/Islamic_inheritance_jurisprudence
- https://en.wikipedia.org/wiki/Labor_theory_of_property
- https://en.wikipedia.org/wiki/History_of_English_land_law
- https://en.wikipedia.org/wiki/Transfer_of_Property_Act_1882

Chapter 5: Transfer of Property Act 1882

In this chapter we discuss the Transfer of Property Act, which consolidates the law in India related to property transfers. The act was made in British India in 1882 and has survived in independent India with a few modifications.

> **THE TRANSFER OF PROPERTY ACT, 1882**
> Act No. 4 of 1882
> [17th February, 1882.]
>
> An Act to amend the law relating to the Transfer of Property by act of Parties.
>
> **Preamble.**—Whereas it is expedient to define and amend certain parts of the law relating to the transfer of property by act of parties; It is hereby enacted as follows:—
>
> CHAPTER I
> PRELIMINARY
>
> **1. Short title.**—This Act may becalled the Transfer of Property Act, 1882.
>
> **Commencements.**—It shallcome into force on the first day of July, 1882.
>
> **Extent.**—[Itextends² in the first instance to the whole of India, except ³[the territories which, immediately before the 1st November, 1956, were comprised in Part B States or in the States of], Bombay, Punjab and Delhi.]
>
> ⁴[But this Act or any part thereof may by ⁵notification in the Official Gazette be extended to the whole or any part of ⁶[the said territories] by the State Government concerned.]
>
> ⁷[And any State Government may, ⁸*** from time to time, by notification in the Official Gazette, exempt, either retrospectively or prospectively, any part of the territories administered by such State Government from all or any of the following provisions, namely:—
>
> Sections 54, paragraphs 2 and 3, 59, 107 and 123.]

Figure: First page of the Transfer of Property Act 1882

5.1 Introduction to the Act

The Transfer of Property Act states the conditions and procedure following which a property can get transferred from one living person to another. Here the legal definition of a "person" can include an individuals, or an association of individuals or a company.

It discusses the different modes of transfer of property including the following:

- sales
- mortgages
- leases
- exchange
- gifts.

In this act, property refers to both moveable as well as immoveable property. Transfer of property, according to the act, is defined as conveying a property by a person to himself or to another living person, including a company or group of individuals, in present or future. The rights, interest, ownership and/or possession of the property can be transferred.

As per the act, any person who is mentally competent and fulfills the other conditions for making a contract can transfer property to another, provided they own the property or are authorized to transfer it. They can transfer it orally or in writing. They can perform the transfer by themselves or by hiring a competent lawyer.

5.2 Conditions for the transfer of property under the Transfer of Property Act

The conditions for transfer are as follows:

- The transfer must be between two living persons
- The property being transferred should be transferable.

    a) It should not have any circumstances in which it cannot be transferred, such as chance of an heir apparent succeeding to an estate.

    b) It should not be a common asset belonging to all, such as the air or sea, that cannot be transferred.

- The person making the transfer should own the property or be competent to transfer it.
- The transfer should be done via a valid method such as sale, exchange, mortgage, lease or gift.
- The transfer cannot be in opposition to the rule of perpetuity. E.g. there should be no condition in the transfer that occurs after infinite time or the lifetime of any of the persons involved.

5.3 Interpretations under the Act

In the act, a few interpretations are stated as follows:

- Immoveable property does not include standing timber, growing crops or grass.
- The transfer must be usually attested by two or more witnesses.

- Transfer of immoveable property should usually be registered under the laws of the state where the property resides.

- A conditional transfer, where the property is transferred upon fulfilment of a condition that is impossible, or dependent on an uncertain future event, or forbidden, or creates injury to some person, is considered to be void and the transfer is invalid.

The act also includes specific amendments for different local laws in different states of India such as Assam and Delhi.

5.4 Types of transfers under the Act

The Transfer of Property act describes different ways in which property can be transferred. For each of these, it describes the transfer and the rights and duties of the parties to the transfer.

The different types of transfer described in the act are as follows:

- **Sale of property**: Sale means a transfer of ownership upon a price paid or promised.

- **Mortgage of immoveable property**: This refers to the transfer of interest in immoveable property as a security for a loan. The act contains detailed instructions on the rights and liabilities of a mortgager and mortgagee, how the mortgage can be redeemed, issues such as foreclosure of a mortgage, how a receiver can be appointed and so on.

- **Lease of immoveable property**: This is the transfer of the rights to enjoy a property for a specified time and upon regular payment of an amount or rent.

- **Exchange**: This is when two persons mutually transfer the ownership of one thing for another or for money only, it is called an exchange.

- **Gift**: Gift is the transfer of moveable or immoveable property by one party, called the donor, to another party called the donee, voluntarily and without any consideration, and accepted by the donee party.

- **Actionable claim**: Transfer of actionable claim means transfer of property upon a claim such as debt, from the debtor to the one they are in debt to, or who has a legally enforceable claim against them.

For each of the above types of transfers, the act lays down the procedure and defines the rights and liabilities of the parties to the transfer.

5.5 Doctrine of Lis Pendens (Section 52)

The doctrine of Lis Pendens ("pending litigation") is outlined in Section 52 of the Transfer of Property Act. It states that if a property is subject to a court dispute, it cannot be legally transferred to another person until the litigation concludes. If someone purchases such property during ongoing litigation, the purchase is subject to the outcome of the lawsuit.

The purpose of this doctrine is to prevent fraudulent transfers and protect parties involved in property litigation. Any transfer done during the period of litigation will be considered subordinate to the rights established by the court's final judgment.

Example:
Suppose Person A and Person B are involved in a lawsuit over ownership of land. If Person A attempts to sell the land to Person C during the court case, the sale is subject to the court's final decision. If Person B wins the case, the transfer to Person C will not affect Person B's rights to the property.

5.6 Doctrine of Part Performance (Section 53A)

Section 53A of the Transfer of Property Act deals with the doctrine of part performance. It provides legal protection to a transferee who has partly performed a contract for the transfer of immovable property.

According to this doctrine, if:

- A valid written contract exists for transfer of immovable property.
- The transferee has taken possession of the property or done an act in furtherance of the contract.
- The transferee has fulfilled their obligations under the contract or is ready and willing to fulfil them.

Then the transferor cannot enforce any right against the transferee concerning the property, except those explicitly provided in the contract.

Example:
Person X agrees to sell a plot of land to Person Y through a valid written contract. Person Y makes a partial payment and takes possession of the property, beginning construction as per the contract terms. Later, Person X tries to reclaim the property. Person Y can use the doctrine of part performance to protect their possession, provided they fulfil their remaining contractual obligations.

5.7 Fraudulent Transfer (Section 53)

The Act also deals with transfers intended to defraud creditors. Under Section 53, any property transfer done intentionally to delay or defraud creditors is voidable at the option of the creditors. However, this will not affect any person who acquired the property in good faith and without knowledge of the fraud, provided consideration was paid for the property.

Example:
Person A owes a substantial debt to Person B. To avoid repayment, Person A transfers their property to a relative, Person C, without receiving proper payment. Person B can challenge this transfer as fraudulent and have it declared void by the court.

5.8 Rule Against Perpetuity (Section 14)

Section 14 of the Transfer of Property Act introduces the rule against perpetuity, which restricts the indefinite transfer of property rights. According to this rule, no property can be transferred in such a way that it suspends the absolute ownership beyond the lifetime of one or more living persons at the time of the transfer plus a period extending to the minority of the unborn beneficiary.

The intention of this rule is to prevent property from being indefinitely tied up and ensure that property remains transferable and commercially viable.

Example:
Person A transfers property to Person B with a condition that after Person B's death, the property will pass on indefinitely to subsequent generations under certain restrictions. Such a condition is void as it violates the rule against perpetuity.

5.9 Difference between Sale and Agreement to Sell

While the Transfer of Property Act covers "sale," it is essential to distinguish clearly between a sale and an agreement to sell:

- **Sale**: Transfer of property ownership occurs immediately, and the buyer obtains immediate rights over the property.
- **Agreement to Sell**: It is a contract indicating an intention to transfer property at a future date upon

the fulfilment of certain conditions. Ownership does not transfer immediately but only when the conditions are fulfilled.

Example:
If Person A transfers a house immediately to Person B against payment, it is a "sale." But if they agree that Person B will buy the house after 6 months upon certain conditions being met, it is an "agreement to sell."

5.10 Importance of Registration and Stamp Duty

While the Transfer of Property Act sets guidelines for property transfer, the Registration Act, 1908, and relevant State Stamp Duty Acts mandate that property transfers must be appropriately stamped and registered. Failure to register certain property transfers, such as sales or leases exceeding one year, makes the transfer legally invalid.

Proper registration ensures:

- Public record of ownership.
- Protection from fraud.
- Admissibility in court as evidence.

Stamp duty rates vary by state and property value, making compliance important for valid property transactions.

5.11 Recent Amendments and Digitalization

In recent years, digital technology has influenced property law significantly. Amendments and government initiatives such as digital stamping, online registration portals, and electronic maintenance of land records have simplified property transactions and improved transparency.

Initiatives such as e-registration, digital land records like Bhulekh, Bhoomi, and similar platforms in various states have streamlined the property transfer process, reducing fraud and simplifying verification.

Chapter 6: Law Related to Sale of Immoveable Property

In this chapter we discuss the law related to sale of immoveable property, under the transfer of property act 1882.

6.1 Definition of sale and contract for sale

Sale is defined as transfer of ownership in exchange for a price paid. A contract for sale is a contract that defines the terms of agreement for sale between the two parties of the sale.

6.2 Rights and Liabilities of buyer and seller

The rights and liabilities defined in the act are applicable for the buyer and seller, in absence of a contract to the contrary.
The rights and liabilities of the seller include:
- The seller is bound to disclose any material defect in the property, to produce documents of title to the buyer, to answer relevant questions, to execute the transfer once the price has been paid, and pay all charges and rent until the day of sale.
- The seller is entitled to the rent and other interests from the property until the day of sale.

The rights and liabilities of the buyer include:

- The buyer is bound to disclose to the seller any interest in the property of which they may not be aware, such as existence of oil beneath the property.
- He is bound to pay the purchase money to the buyer, to bear any loss to the property not caused by the seller, and pay all public charges and rent after the sale is completed.
- The buyer is entitled to benefit from any increase in the value of the property post sale.

6.3 Discharge of incumbrances on sale

Incumbrances here refer to a burden on the property such as a mortgage.

In case the property has a mortgage from a third party who may apply to the court, the court may take part of the proceeds from the sale to pay off the mortgage and any further costs that may be arising and make a direct payment or transfer to the party.

6.4 Rights and Liabilities of Buyer and Seller

When immovable property is transferred by sale, both the buyer and seller have specific legal rights and responsibilities as outlined in the Transfer of Property Act, 1882:

Rights of the Buyer:
- Right to receive the property in good condition as agreed.

- Right to inspect documents of title before completing the transaction.
- Right to peaceful possession of the property.
- Right to claim compensation or damages if defects or encumbrances are discovered later.

Liabilities of the Buyer:
- Duty to pay the agreed price to the seller promptly.
- Responsibility for registration charges and stamp duty unless agreed otherwise.
- Liability to bear losses if damage occurs after possession is transferred unless otherwise specified in the contract.

Rights of the Seller:
- Right to receive payment according to the agreed terms.
- Right to withhold possession until full payment is made if stipulated in the contract.
- Right to compensation for delayed payment or breach of contract by the buyer.

Liabilities of the Seller:
- Duty to disclose defects in title or physical condition of the property.
- Obligation to deliver the property in accordance with the terms agreed.
- Responsibility to ensure the property is free from encumbrances, unless disclosed to the buyer.

6.5 Importance of Clear Title Verification

A critical step in buying immovable property is verifying that the seller has a clear and marketable title. Title verification helps in:
- Confirming the seller's right to sell the property.
- Ensuring the property is free from disputes, mortgages, litigation, or other encumbrances.
- Preventing future disputes or financial loss.

Buyers usually employ legal experts or property consultants to conduct thorough searches and issue title verification reports before finalizing the sale.

6.6 Role of Property Brokers and Agents

Property brokers or agents commonly mediate property transactions. Their role includes:
- Facilitating negotiations between buyers and sellers.
- Assisting in documentation and verification.
- Coordinating with registration authorities and facilitating procedural compliance.

Under RERA (Real Estate Regulatory Authority), brokers dealing with properties in registered projects must also register with the authority and adhere to strict ethical guidelines to protect the interests of buyers.

6.7 Consequences of Breach of Contract in Sale Transactions

When either party breaches the terms of a property sale contract, several remedies are available to the aggrieved party:
- **Damages**: Monetary compensation for loss or harm due to breach.
- **Specific Performance**: Court order compelling the breaching party to fulfil their contractual obligations (for example, completing the sale).
- **Cancellation of Agreement**: The injured party may seek cancellation or rescission of the sale agreement if the breach is significant.

6.8 Sale by Power of Attorney

Occasionally, property transactions occur through a Power of Attorney (PoA), where the owner delegates authority to another person (agent) to act on their behalf:
- **General Power of Attorney (GPA)**: Grants broad powers to handle various property-related matters.
- **Special Power of Attorney (SPA)**: Confined to specific acts, such as selling a particular property.

However, following a landmark Supreme Court ruling (Suraj Lamp & Industries Pvt. Ltd. v. State of Haryana, 2012), sales executed solely via GPA (without proper registration of sale deed) are not considered valid sales. Proper execution and registration of a sale deed is essential for transferring legal ownership.

6.9 Importance of Mutation of Property

Mutation refers to updating government records to reflect the new owner's name after a property transfer. Though mutation itself does not confer ownership, it is crucial because:
- It ensures the property records are up to date for taxation purposes.
- It establishes the proof of ownership in government revenue records.
- It helps the new owner in transactions involving loans or selling the property in the future.

Failure to mutate can create legal complications, making it advisable to promptly complete the mutation process after the registration of the sale deed.

6.10 Digitalization of Sale Transactions and Registrations

In recent years, various Indian states have adopted digital technologies, simplifying property sale transactions and registrations:
- **Online Property Registration**: E-Registration systems reduce paperwork, shorten processing time, and minimize the risk of fraud.
- **Digital Payments**: Payments through online banking, RTGS, or NEFT create documented, traceable transaction histories.
- **E-Stamping**: Facilitates convenient and secure payment of stamp duty, enhancing transparency and ease of doing business.

Such technological advancements have significantly improved efficiency, security, and transparency in property sales.

Chapter 7: Law Related to Mortgage of Property

In this chapter we discuss the sections related to mortgage of immoveable property in the Transfer of Property Act.

7.1 Definition and types of mortgage

Mortgage is the transfer of interest in a property from one party (mortgagor) to another party which is a lender (mortgagee), in exchange for a loan.

For example, the buyer of the property (mortgagor) might have taken a loan from a bank (mortgagee) to pay for the sale.

Mortgage can be of different types.

- Simple mortgage means the person who takes the mortgage undertakes to pay it off by himself.
- Mortgage by conditional sale means the mortgagor sells the property on the condition that if there is a default of the payment by a certain date, then the mortgage will become absolute, but if the payment is made fully, the sale shall become void.
- Usufructuary mortgage means that the mortgagor receives rent and profits from the property until the loan has been fully paid off.
- English mortgage is where the mortgagor binds himself to pay off the mortgage and transfers the property absolutely to the mortgagee, but subject

to the provision that he will re-transfer it back subject to the payment made as agreed.
- Mortgage by deposit of title deeds is where the title deeds are submitted to the creditor in return for the loan.

7.2 Rights and liabilities of the mortgagor

Under the Transfer of Property Act, clear rights and liabilities are outlined for both mortgagors (borrowers) and mortgagees (lenders).

The mortgagor has the right to redeem the property once the loan has been repaid. They have the right to inspect the title deeds and other property documents that have been kept with the mortgagee if needed. They have the right to recover possession upon payment of the debt.

Rights of the Mortgagor (Borrower):
- Right to redeem the property upon repayment of the loan (Right of Redemption).
- Right to inspect and get copies of title deeds deposited with the mortgagee.
- Right to compensation for damage to the property caused by mortgagee's negligence or misuse.

Liabilities of the Mortgagor:
- Responsibility to repay the loan with agreed interest within stipulated time.
- Obligation to maintain and protect the mortgaged property.

- Duty to avoid creating further encumbrances without consent of mortgagee.

7.3 Implied contracts by the mortgagor

There is an implied contract between the mortgagor and mortgagee, which states that:
- the interest which the mortgagor professes to transfer to the mortgagee subsists, and that the mortgagor has power to transfer the same
- the mortgagor will defend, or, if the mortgagee be in possession of the mortgaged property, enable him to defend, the mortgagor's title
- the mortgagor will, so long as the mortgagee is not in possession of the mortgaged property, pay all public charges accruing due in respect of the property
- where the mortgaged property is a lease, that the rent payable under the lease, the conditions contained therein, and the contracts binding on the lessee have been paid, performed and observed down to the commencement of the mortgage

The mortgagor shall also have the power to make leases which shall be binding on the mortgagee.

7.4 Rights and liabilities of the mortgagee (Lender)

The rights of the mortgagee include the following:
- The mortgagee has the right to foreclosure or sale of the property, by getting a suitable decree from

the court, any time after the mortgage money debt is due to him.
- They have the right to sue for mortgage money in case the mortgaged property is wholly or partially destroyed or the security is rendered insufficient without any fault of the mortgagee or mortgager.
- They have the right to appoint a receiver for the mortgaged property.
- If the mortgaged property is on lease that is renewed, then the mortgagee is entitled to the new lease. They have the right to proceeds of the revenue sale in case the mortgager has failed to pay or has arrears.
- Right to retain possession of property documents until repayment.

The liabilities of the mortgagee include the following:
- The mortgagee takes possession of the property during the mortgage and have to manage the property
- They have to collect the rents and profits
- They have to pay taxes on the property
- They have to conduct needed repairs
- They must not commit any destruction on the property.
- Duty to return the title deeds upon full repayment of the loan.
- Obligation to maintain accounts and provide details of loan repayments.

- Responsibility to manage property carefully if possession is taken (e.g., in usufructuary mortgage).

7.5 Miscellaneous items about the mortgage

The mortgagor may deposit the money that is due on the mortgage in court, after which the court may serve a notice of the deposit which, if the mortgagor agrees, will cause the discharge of the mortgage and all the documents of the mortgagor shall be returned. Once the mortgagor has returned the remaining due amount in this way, the interest on the principal money shall cease from that date.

Apart from the mortgagor, other persons with an interest in the property mortgaged, or a creditor of the mortgagor, may file a suit for redemption of the mortgage. For that, they would have the same rights as the mortgagee regarding redemption, foreclosure or sale of the property.

7.6 Sub-Mortgage

A sub-mortgage occurs when a mortgagee (original lender) mortgages their own rights to another lender, effectively creating a second mortgage over the original mortgagee's interest.
- The original borrower's obligations remain unchanged.
- The second lender obtains the rights to collect repayments from the original mortgagee.

- In case of default, the sub-mortgagee can take actions against the original mortgagee, not the mortgagor directly.

This arrangement is less common but is legally recognized and sometimes utilized in complex financial arrangements.

7.7 Priority among Multiple Mortgages

When multiple mortgages are created on the same property, the principle of priority determines which mortgagee has the first claim to repayment in case of default:
- **First Mortgagee**: Has primary rights to repayment. If property is sold, they recover dues first.
- **Subsequent Mortgagees**: Recover their dues from remaining proceeds, if any, after satisfying the first mortgage.

Priority is typically established by date of creation and registration of the mortgage.

7.8 Mortgage by Deposit of Title Deeds (Equitable Mortgage)

Commonly known as an equitable mortgage, this involves depositing original title deeds with the lender as security without a formal registered mortgage deed. Features include:
- Often used by banks and financial institutions due to simpler procedural requirements.

- Must be executed in notified cities and towns (as specified by state governments).
- Stamp duty and registration costs are lower compared to registered mortgages.

It is critical that borrowers clearly document the transaction through a memorandum acknowledging the deposit of title deeds.

7.9 Foreclosure vs Sale of Mortgage Property

The mortgagee's remedy in the event of borrower's default depends on the mortgage type:
- **Foreclosure**: Common in simple mortgages. The lender petitions the court to transfer ownership permanently to them if the borrower defaults, eliminating the borrower's right to redeem the property.
- **Sale of Mortgaged Property**: More common in English mortgages and mortgages with power of sale clauses. Mortgagee sells the property, recovers dues, and returns surplus (if any) to the borrower.

Foreclosure proceedings are strictly regulated and require court intervention, while sale procedures can often be initiated under loan agreement terms without immediate court involvement.

7.10 Charge vs Mortgage

A charge is distinct from a mortgage, although both are security interests created over property:

Introduction to Property Law in India

- **Mortgage**: Involves transfer of interest in specific immovable property as security for repayment.
- **Charge**: Only provides a right of payment from the property but does not transfer ownership or interest. It's merely a security right ensuring the creditor can seek repayment from the property value.

Charges are often created in favour of banks or lenders when the borrower uses property as security without explicitly transferring legal interest.

7.11 Registration and Stamping of Mortgage Deeds

Mortgage deeds generally require compulsory registration under the Registration Act, 1908 (except in equitable mortgages by deposit of title deeds):

- Registered mortgages clearly establish the lender's rights.
- Registration provides evidence admissible in courts, ensuring lender's rights are protected.
- Payment of applicable stamp duty based on loan value is mandatory; rates vary by state.

Failure to register or adequately stamp a mortgage document may render the mortgage unenforceable or invalid.

7.12 Digitalization of Mortgage Transactions

Digital initiatives have streamlined mortgage documentation, registration, and management significantly:

- Online Property Records: Digital land records facilitate easier verification of titles.
- E-stamping and E-registration: Reduces paperwork, cost, and time associated with creating and registering mortgages.
- Central Registry of Securitisation Asset Reconstruction and Security Interest (CERSAI): Helps avoid multiple financing against the same asset by maintaining a centralized record of security interests, reducing fraud.

These digital reforms improve transparency, speed up transactions, and protect lenders and borrowers alike.

Chapter 8: Law Related to Lease of Property

In this chapter we discuss the sections related to lease of immoveable property in the Transfer of Property Act.

8.1 Definition and types of lease

Lease of immoveable property is the transfer of the right to enjoy the property for the fixed and agreed period of time, or in perpetuity, by one party (the lessee) upon payment of a sum of money or some other thing of value to another party (lessor). The sum is called premium.

8.2 How a lease is made

A lease of immoveable property is made by a registered instrument, such as an agreement on registered paper. It can be made from year to year, or a fixed term that is more than a year, upon payment of a fixed amount or yearly rent.

8.3 Rights and liabilities of a lessor and lessee

The rights and liabilities of a lessor include the following:
- A lessor is bound to disclose to the lessee any defects in the property before the lease is agreed.

- As long as the lessee follows the contract on the lease, they can hold the property for the time of the lease without interruption.

8.4 Rights and Liabilities of Lessor and Lessee

Under the Transfer of Property Act, 1882, clear rights and liabilities are defined for both lessors (landlords) and lessees (tenants):

Rights of the Lessor (Landlord):
- Right to receive rent in accordance with the lease agreement.
- Right to recover possession of property at the end of the lease period.
- Right to inspect the leased property periodically, subject to reasonable notice.
- Right to terminate the lease and evict the lessee in case of breach of lease terms.

Liabilities of the Lessor:
- Duty to disclose any known material defects in the property.
- Obligation to allow the lessee peaceful possession and enjoyment without interference.
- Responsibility for structural repairs unless specified otherwise in the lease agreement.

The rights and liabilities of the lessee include the following:

- If the property is destroyed by natural cause or fire or war, the lease shall become void.

Rights of the Lessee (Tenant):
- Right to peaceful and uninterrupted possession during the lease term.
- Right to sub-lease or assign the lease, unless specifically restricted in the agreement.
- Right to enjoy the leased property without interference from the landlord.
- If the lessor does not make needed repairs to the property, the lessee may make the same and deduct its costs from the rent.

Liabilities of the Lessee:
- The lessee is bound to pay on time the rent or premium agreed to the lessor.
- Duty to maintain and use the property in a responsible manner.
- The lessee is bound to restore the property to its original state on termination of the lease, barring any reasonable wear and tear.
- The lessee should not insert any permanent construction on the property without the lessor's consent.
- Responsibility to return the property in good condition (subject to normal wear and tear) after expiry or termination of the lease.

8.5 Sub-Lease and Assignment of Lease

A lessee sometimes creates a further lease of the leased property. This is called a sub-lease:

- Sub-Lease: The lessee (original tenant) grants a lease to another tenant, called the sub-lessee. The lessee retains responsibilities towards the lessor (original landlord).
- Assignment of Lease: The lessee transfers all rights and obligations under the lease to another party, making the new party directly liable to the lessor.

Typically, lease agreements specifically address whether sub-leasing or assignment is permissible.

8.6 Determination (Termination) of Lease

A lease may end or terminate through several methods:

- Expiry of Lease Term: Lease automatically ends upon completion of the fixed lease period.
- Notice to Quit: In leases with no fixed period (e.g., monthly tenancy), termination occurs upon serving notice.
- Mutual Agreement: The parties may mutually decide to end the lease before its term.
- Forfeiture: Landlord terminates lease due to breach of conditions by tenant.
- Surrender: Tenant voluntarily returns property, and landlord accepts termination.

Clear procedures must be followed for termination to be legally effective.

8.7 Lease vs License

Lease and license are two different legal arrangements concerning property occupation:

- Lease: Transfers exclusive possession and interest in property for a specified period. Lessee has rights protected under law and cannot be evicted arbitrarily.
- License: Merely grants a permission to use property temporarily without transferring possession or interest. Licenses are revocable at the licensor's discretion.

Example: Renting a flat for one year constitutes a lease. Allowing someone temporary access to property for hosting an event constitutes a license.

8.8 Registration and Stamp Duty Requirements for Lease

Leases exceeding one year are required by law to be compulsorily registered under the Registration Act, 1908:

- Registration provides legal validity and admissibility as evidence.
- Lease agreements attract stamp duty, varying across states depending on lease tenure and rental value.
- Short-term leases (below one year) may not require mandatory registration but may still attract nominal stamp duty as per state laws.

8.9 Impact of RERA on Lease Agreements

The Real Estate (Regulation and Development) Act, 2016 (RERA) primarily governs property sales but indirectly affects leases:
- Residential leases in RERA-approved projects must adhere to transparency norms regarding property details.
- Developers leasing apartments or units must clearly disclose the status and details of approvals, possession dates, and facilities.

RERA enhances transparency, indirectly benefiting lessees by ensuring project compliance and reliability of disclosed information.

8.10 Rights of Lessees in Case of Property Sale

If leased property is sold to another party during an ongoing lease, the lessee generally retains their rights:
- New owner must honour existing leases unless explicitly stated otherwise.
- Tenants cannot be forced out arbitrarily; new owners must abide by agreed lease terms and duration.

Lease agreements often explicitly outline procedures if the property changes ownership.

8.11 Lease Disputes and Legal Remedies

Common lease disputes include eviction, failure to pay rent, damages, or breach of lease terms. Legal remedies available are:
- Suit for Eviction: Landlord files suit to recover possession due to tenant's default or lease expiration.

- Suit for Recovery of Rent or Damages: Landlord may sue tenants who default on rent or damage the property.
- Injunction or Stay Orders: Tenants may seek court injunctions against illegal eviction attempts or harassment.

Rent Control Tribunals, Civil Courts, and Consumer Forums handle such disputes based on jurisdiction and lease type.

8.12 Digital Lease Registration and Documentation

Digitization initiatives simplify lease registration and compliance:

- E-registration portals allow easy registration of lease agreements, significantly reducing processing time.
- Online rent payment and digital receipts ensure transparent record-keeping.
- Digital platforms help landlords and tenants verify documents quickly, reducing disputes.

Such technological improvements benefit both lessors and lessees by enhancing efficiency, clarity, and ease of property transactions.

Chapter 9: Law Related to Exchange of Property

In this chapter we discuss the sections related to exchange of immoveable property in the Transfer of Property Act.

9.1 Definition of exchange

Exchange of immoveable property is a transaction when two persons mutually transfer the ownership of one thing for another thing, or for money only.

9.2 Rights and liabilities of the parties in exchange

Both the parties have the same rights and liabilities as that of seller in a sale in respect of what they give, and buyer in a sale with what they take.
If the exchange is of money, each party has to show the genuineness of the money given.

9.3 Essential Elements of a Valid Exchange

To constitute a valid exchange under the Transfer of Property Act, 1882, the following elements must be satisfied:
- Mutual Consent: Both parties must voluntarily agree to the exchange without coercion, undue influence, or fraud.

- Existence of Property: Both properties involved in the exchange must exist and be clearly identifiable.
- Legal Competence: Both parties must be legally competent (of sound mind, majority age, and not disqualified by law) to transfer their properties.
- Lawful Consideration: The properties exchanged must have lawful consideration, meaning they cannot be properties that are illegal or prohibited from being transferred.
- No Monetary Consideration Required: Unlike a sale, exchange does not necessarily involve monetary consideration; the consideration is another property.

9.4 Rights and Liabilities of Parties in Exchange

In an exchange transaction, the Transfer of Property Act specifies rights and liabilities similar to a sale transaction:

Rights of Parties:
- Right to receive the property in the agreed condition.
- Right to peaceful and uninterrupted possession of the exchanged property.
- Right to clear title free from encumbrances unless otherwise explicitly stated.

Liabilities of Parties:

- Obligation to disclose any known defects or encumbrances on the property.
- Responsibility to deliver possession and clear title as agreed.
- Liability for losses arising from defects or encumbrances undisclosed at the time of exchange.

9.5 Exchange vs. Sale

It is important to clearly differentiate between exchange and sale:

Exchange	Sale
Property is exchanged for property	Property is exchanged for money
Both parties are simultaneously buyers and sellers	Distinct buyer and seller roles
Requires mutual transfer of property rights	Requires payment of monetary consideration

Understanding these differences helps avoid disputes regarding the nature and legal implications of property transactions.

9.6 Stamp Duty and Registration Requirements in Exchange

An exchange of immovable properties is treated similarly to a sale concerning stamp duty and registration:

- Registration is compulsory under the Registration Act, 1908, for exchanges involving immovable properties valued above ₹100.
- Stamp Duty: Payable based on the value of the property with the higher market valuation among the exchanged properties. Stamp duty rates differ across states and must be calculated carefully.

Non-registration or inadequate stamping can result in the invalidation of the exchange and may affect legal rights of the parties involved.

9.7 Tax Implications in Exchange Transactions

Exchange transactions have distinct tax implications:
- Capital Gains Tax: Exchange of immovable property is subject to capital gains tax. Each party pays tax based on the difference between the acquisition cost and the fair market value of the exchanged property.
- Valuation: Tax authorities may assess the market value of exchanged properties to determine tax liability.
- Exemptions: Specific exemptions or deductions may be available under income tax law if the transaction meets certain criteria or reinvestment conditions.

Consulting tax professionals before finalizing an exchange is highly advisable.

9.8 Exchange under Personal Laws

Property exchange under personal laws (such as Hindu or Muslim law) may differ in certain details:
- Under Hindu Law, exchanges typically follow general principles outlined in the Transfer of Property Act.
- Under Islamic Law, an exchange is termed "Hiba bil Iwaz", involving giving property in exchange for property, governed by principles of Muslim personal law.

Awareness of these variations is important when parties are governed by personal laws.

9.9 Precautions Before Entering into an Exchange

Before finalizing an exchange transaction, the following precautions are recommended:
- Verify Title: Ensure both properties have clear, dispute-free titles.
- Valuation: Independently assess the market values of properties to avoid unfair deals or taxation issues.
- Written Agreement: Clearly document all terms, conditions, and representations in a written and registered exchange deed.
- Legal Advice: Obtain professional legal and financial advice to manage risks, tax obligations, and legal compliance effectively.

9.10 Remedies for Breach of Exchange Agreement

In case of breach or non-performance by any party in an exchange transaction, the following legal remedies are available:
- Specific Performance: Court order directing the defaulting party to fulfil obligations agreed in the exchange.
- Rescission or Cancellation: Court-directed cancellation of the agreement if significant breaches or fraudulent practices occur.
- Damages: Monetary compensation for losses incurred due to breach of the agreement.

These remedies help safeguard the rights and interests of both parties in property exchanges.

9.11 Digital and Technological Impact on Exchange Transactions

With digital advancements:
- Online Registration: Digital portals allow for streamlined and transparent registration of exchange agreements, significantly reducing processing time.
- Digital Document Verification: Facilitates quick verification of property titles and valuation, minimizing fraud risk.
- E-stamping: Simplifies stamp duty payment, creating an efficient and secure record of property transactions.

These digital improvements are essential for making exchange transactions transparent, efficient, and secure.

Chapter 10: Laws Related to Gift of Property

In this chapter we discuss the sections related to gifts of immoveable property in the Transfer of Property Act.

10.1 Introduction to gifts

Gift is the transfer of certain property without any consideration or payment. It is made by one person (donor) to another (donee) and accepted by the donee.

For a gift to be valid, the transfer has to be affected on a registered instrument signed by the donor, and attested by at least two witnesses. The gift must be of existing property, not future property.

A gift can be suspended or revoked only in certain cases, such as when if it were a contract, the contract could be rescinded.

In case of a gift, the donee cannot accept part of the gift, he has to accept the whole gift or take nothing of it.

10.2 Revocation of Gift

Generally, once a gift of property has been legally completed, it cannot be revoked. However, under specific conditions provided by law, revocation may still be permissible:

- Mutual Agreement: Both donor and donee agree to revoke the gift voluntarily.

Introduction to Property Law in India

- Conditional Gifts: If a gift was conditional and the donee fails to fulfil the agreed conditions, the gift may be revoked.
- Fraud or Undue Influence: If a gift was made due to coercion, fraud, misrepresentation, or undue influence, the donor can seek revocation through legal action.

A mere change of mind or regret by the donor does not justify revocation.

10.3 Conditional Gifts

Sometimes, gifts are made subject to certain conditions. These conditions could either precede (conditions precedent) or follow (conditions subsequent) the gift:

- Conditions Precedent: Gift becomes valid only if specific conditions are met by the donee.
- Conditions Subsequent: Gift is initially valid but can be revoked if conditions are later breached or unfulfilled.

Example:

A father gifts property to his daughter on the condition that she completes higher education. If she fails to fulfil this condition, the father may revoke the gift.

10.4 Tax Implications of Gift Transactions

Gifts, particularly of immovable property, have significant tax implications under Indian Income Tax laws:

- Gifts of immovable property exceeding ₹50,000 in value received by non-relatives are taxable in the hands of the recipient as "Income from Other Sources".
- Stamp Duty Valuation: If the stamp duty value exceeds the declared value by more than 10%, the difference is taxed as income.
- Exemptions: Gifts from close relatives (e.g., spouse, parents, siblings), on marriage, inheritance, or from registered charitable organizations are exempt from tax.

Therefore, careful consideration of tax liabilities is crucial before gifting property.

10.5 Gifts Under Personal Laws

Personal laws in India can influence how gifts are handled:

Hindu Law (Under Hindu Succession Act and personal customs):
- No specific restrictions apart from general legal principles.
- A Hindu can gift their self-acquired property freely; ancestral property gifts are restricted and may require consent of coparceners.

Muslim Law (Hiba):

- Oral gifts (hiba) are permissible if accompanied by immediate delivery of possession and acceptance by donee.
- Writing and registration of gift deeds, though recommended, is not mandatory under Muslim personal law.

Understanding these variations helps in correctly executing and validating gifts as per applicable personal laws.

10.6 Rights and Liabilities of Donor and Donee

The Transfer of Property Act defines clear rights and obligations regarding gifts:

Rights of Donor:
- Right to freely transfer property through gifting, provided it is legally permissible and voluntarily done.
- Right to revoke the gift under specific conditions as discussed above.

Liabilities of Donor:
- Obligation to deliver possession and title documents immediately to the donee.
- Duty to disclose material defects or encumbrances on the gifted property at the time of gifting.

Rights of Donee:

- Right to immediate and peaceful possession and enjoyment of gifted property.
- Right to receive clear title and all relevant documentation from the donor.

Liabilities of Donee:
- Obligation to accept the gift explicitly; non-acceptance invalidates the gift.
- Responsibility to fulfil any valid conditions attached to the gift.

10.7 Importance of Acceptance in Gifts
A crucial requirement for a valid gift under the Transfer of Property Act is the acceptance of the gift by the donee. Acceptance must be:
- Voluntary and not induced by fraud or coercion.
- Explicitly communicated or clearly implied through acts (e.g., occupying or utilizing the gifted property).

A gift without clear acceptance from the donee is incomplete and legally invalid.

10.8 Gift vs. Will
Though similar, gifts and wills are legally distinct methods of transferring property:

Gift	Will
Immediate transfer of ownership	Transfer occurs after the death of the testator
Irrevocable (generally)	Revocable and alterable any number of times
Requires acceptance by donee	Acceptance by beneficiaries required only after death
Effective immediately upon execution	Effective only after death and probate (if applicable)

Choosing between gifting or writing a will depends on personal circumstances, immediate needs, and long-term family planning goals.

10.9 Remedies for Fraudulent or Improper Gifts

If a gift transaction involves fraud, coercion, undue influence, or illegality, several remedies are available:
- Revocation or Cancellation: Courts can revoke or cancel a gift proven to have been procured through unlawful means.
- Injunctions: Preventive court orders can be obtained to stop misuse or illegal transfer following a fraudulent gift.
- Restoration or Compensation: Donees may be ordered to restore property or compensate the donor if the gift was improperly procured.

Legal action can be pursued through civil courts or competent authorities, depending on the circumstances.

Chapter 11: Indian Succession Act 1925

In this chapter we discuss the Indian Succession Act 1925, which governs the transfer of moveable as well as immoveable property through inheritance or succession upon one's death.

The Indian Succession Act was made in British Indian in 1925, and has generally survived as such after Indian independence with some subsequent amendments hence.

11.1 Indian Succession Act 1925

The Indian Succession Act 1925 is an act to consolidate the law applicable to intestate (dying without a will) and testamentary succession (succession where a will is present). The purpose of this law is to present the whole body of statutory law on the subject of wills and succession in a complete form.

The ordinary meaning of the word "succession" is a transmission by law or by the will of the man to one or more persons of the property and transmission rights and obligations of a deceased person. The federal court gave its opinion on a reference in the matter of the powers of the federal legislature to provide for the levy of an estate duty in respect of property other than agricultural land, passing upon the death of any person [AIR 1944 FC 73].

Introduction to Property Law in India

> THE INDIAN SUCCESSION ACT, 1925
> ACT NO. 39 OF 1925[1]
>
> [30th September, 1925.]
>
> An Act to consolidate the law applicable to intestate and testamentary succession [2]***.
>
> WHEREAS it is expedient to consolidate the law applicable to intestate and testamentary succession [2]***. It is hereby enacted as follows:—
>
> PART I
> PRELIMINARY
>
> **1. Short title.**—This Act may be called the Indian Succession Act, 1925.
>
> **2. Definitions.**—In this Act, unless there is anything repugnant in the subject or context,—
>
> (a) "administrator" means a person appointed by competent authority to administer the estate of a deceased person when there is no executor;
>
> (b) "codicil" means an instrument made in relation to a Will, and explaining, altering or adding to its dispositions, and shall be deemed to form part of the Will;
>
> [3][(bb) "District Judge" means the Judge of a Principal Civil Court of original jurisdiction;]
>
> (c) "executor" means a person to whom the execution of the last Will of a deceased person is, by the testator's appointment, confided;
>
> [4][(cc) "India" means the territory of India excluding the State of Jammu and Kashmir;]
>
> (d) "Indian Christian" means a native of India who is, or in good faith claims to be, of unmixed Asiatic descent and who professes any form of the Christian religion;

Figure: First page of the Indian Succession Act 1925

The law of succession is the law governing the transmission of property vested in a person at his death to some other person or persons.

The act discusses the cases in which a person can die with or without making a will:

- A person dies intestate i.e. without making a will, and how their moveable and immoveable property can be divided among their various heirs starting from the closest relatives such as widow and children.

- Testamentary succession, i.e. where the deceased person has left a will before they died, specifying exactly how their property can be divided and among whom.

11.2 Summary of the act

The Indian succession act covers different grounds related to wills and other aspects of succession.

It discusses who can and cannot make a will, what is a valid will, different types of bequests, how an administrator can be appointed, how probate and letters of succession can be granted, how debts, legacies and gifts are to be paid and so on. It also covers different state amendments.

11.3 Characteristics of a will

The essential characteristics of a will are as follows:

- There must be a legal declaration of the testator's (the person making the will) intention
- The declaration must be with respect to the property of the testator
- The declaration must be to the effect that it is to operate after the death of the testator i.e. it should be revocable during the life of the testator.
- It lists the moveable and immoveable assets and states how and among whom the assets are to be divided and in what ratio

- The will must be signed and attested by two witnesses.

A will may contain the following components (as a guideline):

- A declaration by the person that this is the last will and all previous wills are invalid
- A declaration that the person is in good health and mind, and is making the will of his own free choice
- Name of the survivors (wife and children)
- Description of the person's moveable and immoveable property
- How the assets are to be divided in in whose names
- Signature of the person with date
- Name and Signature of two witnesses

Introduction to Property Law in India

```
┌─────────────────────────────────────┐
│ Declaration that this is the last will │
│    and previous wills are invalid      │
└─────────────────────────────────────┘
┌─────────────────────────────────────┐
│ Declaration that the person is in good │
│ health and mind, and is making the will│
│    of their own free choice            │
└─────────────────────────────────────┘
┌─────────────────────────────────────┐
│  Names of the survivors (wife and     │
│         children etc.)                 │
└─────────────────────────────────────┘
┌─────────────────────────────────────┐
│  List of moveable and immoveable      │
│              property                  │
└─────────────────────────────────────┘
┌─────────────────────────────────────┐
│  Description of how the assets are to │
│            be divided                  │
└─────────────────────────────────────┘
┌─────────────────────────────────────┐
│   Signature of the person with date   │
└─────────────────────────────────────┘
┌─────────────────────────────────────┐
│   Names and Signatures of two         │
│            witnesses                   │
└─────────────────────────────────────┘
```

Figure: Illustration of the components of a will

11.4 Understanding the testator's intention

To ascertain the intention of the testator while making a will, the court is concerned with three distinct questions:

- What words has the testator used to express his intention

- What is the meaning of such words in relation to the persons and the things described; and

- What is the meaning of the words in relation to the disposition of such property among the donee(s)

When the intention of the testator has been discovered, the next enquiry by the court should be to ascertain whether there is any rule preventing the intention from taking effect and how the intention can be effectuated (Halisbury law).

11.5 Probate of a will

Probate is the legal procedure in which the deceased person's property is examined and evaluated, claims against the estate are paid and the remaining property is distributed:

- to the heirs if there is a will or
- according to intestacy / state law if no will is present

Probate is also the name given to the petition to the court for granting the authority to an executor to execute the will of a testator.

Probate of a will, when granted, establishes the will from the death of the testator and renders valid all intermediate acts of the executor as such.

Probate is conclusive as to the genuineness of the will and appointment of executors.

Once probate is granted, no suit will lie for a declaration that the testator was not of a sound mind.

Probate is conclusive as to the representative title of the executor against the debtors of the deceased and gives complete indemnity to them, as per Section 273 of ISA 1925.

As the executor derives his title under the will and all the properties of the testator vest in him immediately on the death of the testator, on the grant of probate, all his intermediate acts in connection with the estate are validated [AIR 1956 Mod 274]. This section enacts that the vesting takes place on the taking of probate but relates back to the time of the testator's death and to the estate which then belonged to him. Under Section 221 of ISA 1925, in the case of an administrator only those acts which are beneficial to the estate and validated by the grant are validated.

A probate petition should contain the following details:

- Details of the deceased and their legal heirs
- Details of the will, including date and circumstances of death
- Details of the property of the deceased
- Statement that the petitioners are the sole heirs as per the will and undertake to pay the duties
- Prayer to grant probate
- Affidavit of the petitioners

```
┌─────────────────────────────────────────────┐
│ Details of the **deceased and legal heirs** │
└─────────────────────────────────────────────┘
┌─────────────────────────────────────────────┐
│ Details of the **will**, date and circumstances │
│                  of death                   │
└─────────────────────────────────────────────┘
┌─────────────────────────────────────────────┐
│ Details of the **property** of the deceased │
└─────────────────────────────────────────────┘
┌─────────────────────────────────────────────┐
│ **Statement** that the petitioners are heirs and │
│       undertake to pay their duties         │
└─────────────────────────────────────────────┘
┌─────────────────────────────────────────────┐
│        **Prayer** to grant probate          │
└─────────────────────────────────────────────┘
┌─────────────────────────────────────────────┐
│        **Affidavit** of the petitioners     │
└─────────────────────────────────────────────┘
```

Figure: Illustration of the components of a probate petition or application

The court procedure for probate of a will is as follows:

- The petitioners submit the probate application at an appropriate court in the prescribed format, along with the accompanying documents such as death certificate, affidavits and court fees
- Court receives the application and verifies the details
- Court directs to publish in leading newspapers a notice inviting the members of the public and next of kin of the deceased to file any objections. It also directs to send notification letters to the next of kin

at their addresses mentioned in the probate application, informing them of the application of probate.

- If after a period of time, there is no objection, the court issues the probate and letters of administration, upon payment of the court fees (which depend on the value of the assets).

- If there is an objection from one or more of the parties, the issuance of probate is delayed. The normal court procedure takes place, with presentation of evidence, arguments and cross examination from the parties. After examining the evidence and arguments, the court issues its judgment regarding the grant of probate and letters of administration.

11.6 Proving genuineness of a will and suspicious circumstances

To prove the genuineness of the will in a court of law, the propounder must prove five things:

- The testamentary capacity of the testator, i.e., of the person making the will

- The testamentary nature of the instrument, i.e., that the will does not dispose of any property in present but only on the death of the executant

- The testator's knowledge of the contents of the instrument and his approval of the same.

- The absence of undue influence, fraud etc.
- Due execution by the testator and its attestation by witnesses as required by law.

The list of suspicious circumstances surrounding a will can include the following:

- Signature of the testator may be shaky and doubtful.
- The condition of the testator's mind may appear to be feeble and debilitated.
- Mental capacity of the testator may be doubtful.
- The dispositions made in the will may appear to be unnatural, improbable or unfair.
- The will may otherwise indicate that the said dispositions may not be the result of the testator's free will of mind.
- Exercise of undue influence, fraud or coercion can be shown in respect of execution of will.
- the propounder of the will themselves takes a prominent part in the execution of the will which confers on them substantial benefit.

11.7 Validity of a will obtained by coercion or undue influence

If it is proved that a will is obtained by dubious means such as coercion, fraud or undue influence, such a will is ruled to be invalid. Some instances include the following:

- **Coercion**: Whatever destroys the free agency of the testator constitutes coercion. If actual force was used to compel the testator to make the will and all the formalities are complied with, yet the will is void [1 Cox 355]. Examples of coercion include threat to suicide by any of the parties, in order to compel the testator to include them in their will.

- **Undue influence**: Undue influence is the improper use of power or trust in a way that deprives a person of free will and substitutes another's objective [Black's Law Dictionary: 8th Edition]. It is any kind of influence that takes away the free agency of the testator.

- **Unsound mind**: If at the time of making the will the testator is proven to have unsound mind, that will is proven to be invalid. Unsoundness of mind may be occasioned by physical infirmity or advancing years as distinguished from mental derangement and the resulting defeat of intelligence may be the cause of incapacity, but the intelligence must be reduced to such an extent that the proposed testator does not appreciate the testamentary act in all its bearings. Old age or the near approach of death at any age, lend strength to the suggestion that the testator had proper knowledge of the contents of the will [Williams, Law of Wills pp. 20-21].

To prove a will is valid, the propounder of the will has to show that the will was signed by the testator, that he was at the relevant time in a sound disposing state of mind, that he understood the nature and the effect of the dispositions, that he had signed in the presence of two witnesses who attested it in his presence and in the presence of each other. Once these elements are established, the onus which rests on the propounder is discharged [Surendra Pal v Dr. Sarswati AIR 1974 SC 1999].

11.8 Format of a sample will

The format of a sample will is as follows:

I, <name of testator>, son of <father's name>, aged <age in years>, resident of <address of testator>, declare this to be my last will and testament. This will cancels all my prior wills made by me.

I am in good health and possess a good mind. This will was made independently by me. No one has influenced or compelled me to make this will.

I hereby appoint <name of executor>, as the sole executor of this will.

My wife's name is <name of wife>. We have <number of children> children, whose names are as follows:

1.

2.

I have the following immovable and movable property:

1. A flat in the address _____

2. Jewelry, shares in various companies, cash and cash in bank accounts.

I declare that all the above assets are owned by me, and I have full authority over these assets.

I entrust all my movable and immovable properties to the following persons in the following ways

1. I give my bank account to my wife

2. I give my flat in the name of my son

(   )

Testator's signature

Date

Signed by the testator as a last will in our presence. We have fully understood and approved the material and have signed our names as witnesses in the presence of the testator and in the presence of each other.

Name and signature of witnesses:

1.(name and signature of witness)

2. (name and signature of witness)

11.9 Format of a sample probate petition for a will

A sample petition for probate is as follows:

IN THE COURT OF _____

Probate case No. __ of __<year>

In the matter of

Mr __ <petitioner name>

Resident of ___ (Petitioner)

verses

State   (Respondents)

Probate petition under section 276 of the Indian Succession Act on behalf of the petitioners for grant of probate in respect of the will dated ___ executed by ___ son of ___ resident of ___ in favour of the petitioners namely __.

MOST RESPECTFULLY SHOWETH:

1. That ___, son of ___, resident of ___, hereafter known as the deceased, who was a Hindu governed by the Hindu Succession Act, died on ___ at ___, which was his fixed place of residence. A copy of the death certificate issued by the sub registrar of births and deaths is annexed herewith as Annexure A.

2. That at the time of death, the deceased was about __ years of age. During his life time, the deceased duly executed a will dated __ in respect of moveable and immoveable property bearing ___.

3. That at the time of death, the deceased left behind the following legal heirs:

i) name, address, age, relationship

ii) name, address, age, relationship

iii) name, address, age, relationship

4. That prior to his death, the deceased executed the will dated ___ in favour of ___ and ___

5. That the deceased was competent to execute the will dated ___, being the owner of the property at ___ having the following details:

6. That it is submitted that through the said will, the deceased bequeathed the said property in the following manner:

i)

ii)

iii)

7. That the petitioners after the death of ___ became the sole executors/legal heirs of the deceased testator as per the will in respect of the property mentioned herein above.

8. That late ___ was residing in ___, died in ___ on the date ___. Further the property left behind by the deceased was situated in ___, which is within the jurisdiction of this honourable court.

9. That the will dated ___ is annexed to the affidavit of ___, who is one of the attesting witnesses.

10. That the value of the assets of said deceased beyond the limit of the State of __ does not exceed Rs. ___.

11. That to the best of the petitioner's knowledge, no application has been made to any High Court or other District Court for probate of the said will.

12. That the petitioner undertakes to pay the duty payable for the grant of probate.

PRAYER

The petitioner therefore most respectfully prays that in the facts and circumstances of the case the probate in respect of the will dated ___ executed by late ___ be granted in favour of the petitioners, in the interest of justice.

For such other order/relief/direction as this honourable court may deem just and proper be also passed in favour of the petitioners.

AFFIDAVIT

I, ___, son of ___, aged ___, resident of ___, do hereby solemnly affirm and declare as under:

1. That I am the petitioner no. 1 and am well conversant with the facts of the case.

2. That the facts stated in the accompanying petition have been drafted by our counsel under my instructions which are all true and correct.

(Signed)

At:

Dated:

Chapter 12: Sale of Goods Act 1930

In this chapter we go through the Sale of Goods Act of 1930, which defines the law related to the sale of goods and transfer of ownership, including moveable property but not land. It mainly focuses on contracts between the buyers and sellers.

Even though the act does not consider land, but many moveable items sold along with property could be included in this act. That is why we are discussing this act as well.

THE SALE OF GOODS ACT, 1930
ACT NO. 3 OF 1930[1]

[15th March, 1930.]

An Act to define and amend the law relating to the sale of goods.

WHEREAS it is expedient to define and amend the law relating to the sale of goods; It is hereby enacted as follows:—

CHAPTER I

PRELIMINARY

1. Short title, extent and commencement.—(1) This Act may be called the [2]*** Sale of Goods Act, 1930.

[3][(2) It extends to the whole of India [4][except the State of Jammu and Kashmir].]

(3) It shall come into force on the 1st day of July, 1930.

2. Definitions.—In this Act, unless there is anything repugnant in the subject or context,—

(1) "buyer" means a person who buys or agrees to buy goods;

(2) "delivery" means voluntary transfer of possession from one person to another;

(3) goods are said to be in a "deliverable state" when they are in such state that the buyer would under the contract be bound to take delivery of them;

(4) "document of title to goods" includes a bill of lading, dockwarrant, warehouse keeper's certificate, wharfingers' certificate, railway receipt, [5][multimodal transport document,] warrant or order for the delivery of goods and any other document used in the ordinary course of business as proof of the possession or control of goods, or authorising or purporting to authorise, either by endorsement or by delivery, the possessor of the document to transfer or receive goods thereby

Figure: First page of the Sale of Goods Act 1930

12.1 Summary of the Act

The Sale of Goods Act 1930 defines a contract for a sale of goods between a buyer and a seller, where the ownership of an item is transferred from the seller to the buyer upon payment of a price.

In the act, the term "goods" refers to "*every kind of movable property other than actionable claims and money; and includes stock and shares, growing crops, grass, and things attached to or forming part of the land which are agreed to be severed before sale or under the contract of sale.*"

Along with the ownership and rights, any risks and liabilities associated with the item are also transferred from the seller to the buyer. The act covers existing goods as well as goods to be transferred in the future.

The act defines what is a contract of sale and the various conditions associated with the contract. It also covers various cases where the goods are faulty or the contract conditions are not met. It covers the rights of the buyers and the sellers, as well as special conditions like damaged goods and auctions.

12.2 Conditions for a valid sale

The conditions for a valid contract for sale include the following:
- The sale must be between at least two parties
- The subject matter of the sale must be goods to be sold. It is not, for example, a contract to perform some work.
- A consideration, such as money, must be paid for the sale

- The delivery and transfer of the ownership of goods sold must take place from the seller to the buyer.

12.3 Rights and Duties of Buyer and Seller under the Sale of Goods Act

The Sale of Goods Act 1930 defines specific duties and rights for both parties in a sale of goods transaction. Understanding these is important for resolving disputes and ensuring fair dealings.

Duties of the Seller:
- To deliver the goods according to the terms of the contract.
- To transfer the right of ownership to the buyer upon completion of the sale.
- To ensure that the goods sold correspond to their description (implied condition of description).
- To warrant that the goods are free from any undisclosed charges or encumbrances in favour of third parties (implied warranty of quiet possession).

Rights of the Buyer:
- Right to inspect the goods before accepting delivery.
- Right to reject goods that do not conform to the contract terms or are not of satisfactory quality.
- Right to claim damages or repudiate the contract if the seller is in breach of a condition of the sale.

12.4 Implied Conditions and Warranties

The Sale of Goods Act 1930 incorporates certain implied conditions and warranties into every contract of sale, unless expressly excluded by the parties. A condition is a fundamental term whose breach gives the aggrieved party the right to repudiate (cancel) the contract, whereas a warranty is a lesser term whose breach only gives rise to a claim for damages.

Key Implied Conditions include:
- **Condition as to Title:** In a sale, the seller has the right to sell the goods; in an agreement to sell, the seller will have that right at the time of transfer. If a seller sells goods without having title, the buyer can return them and get a refund even after use.
- **Sale by Description:** Where goods are sold by description, there is an implied condition that the goods shall correspond to that description. For example, if a buyer orders a particular model of a washing machine, the seller must supply exactly that model.
- **Condition as to Quality or Fitness:** Where the buyer expressly or by implication makes known to the seller the particular purpose for which the goods are required, there is an implied condition that the goods shall be reasonably fit for that purpose. For example, if a buyer tells a hardware shop owner that they need a drill capable of drilling through concrete, the goods supplied must be fit for that specific purpose.
- **Condition in Sale by Sample:** Where goods are sold by sample, the bulk of the goods must correspond with the sample in quality; the buyer must have a reasonable opportunity of comparing the bulk with the sample; and the goods must be

free from any defect rendering them unmerchantable that would not be apparent on reasonable examination of the sample.

12.5 Transfer of Property and Risk in Goods

Under the Sale of Goods Act 1930, the passing of property (ownership) in goods is a critical concept, as it determines who bears the risk if the goods are lost, damaged, or destroyed. The general rule is that risk follows ownership — the party who owns the goods bears the risk of loss at any given time.

The Act distinguishes between specific goods (goods identified and agreed upon at the time of making the contract) and unascertained goods (goods not specifically identified at the time of sale but which form part of a general category). Property in specific goods passes when the parties intend it to pass. Property in unascertained goods passes only when the goods are ascertained and appropriated to the contract with the consent of both parties.

Example: Mr. A buys a specific television set displayed in a shop window. The property in the TV passes immediately when the contract is agreed upon, even before delivery. If the shop catches fire overnight and the TV is destroyed, the risk is with Mr. A who is already the owner, and he cannot demand a refund from the seller.

12.6 Unpaid Seller and Remedies

An unpaid seller is one who has not received the full price for the goods sold, or who has received a negotiable instrument (like a cheque) that has not yet been honoured. An unpaid seller has several special rights

under the Act, even after property has passed to the buyer:
- **Right of Lien:** The right to retain possession of the goods until the price is paid. This applies where the goods have been sold without any stipulation as to credit, or on credit that has expired.
- **Right of Stoppage in Transit:** Where the buyer becomes insolvent and the goods are in transit (not yet in the buyer's possession), the seller may stop the goods and resume possession until payment is made.
- **Right of Resale:** If the goods are of a perishable nature, or if the seller gives notice of his intention to resell and the buyer still does not pay, the seller has a right to resell the goods. If the resale price is lower, the seller can claim the difference from the buyer as damages.

12.7 Sale by Auction

The Act has special provisions concerning the sale of goods by auction. An auction sale is a public sale where goods are sold to the highest bidder. The following rules govern auction sales:
- Where goods are put up for sale in lots, each lot is prima facie (on the face of it) deemed to be a separate contract of sale.
- The sale is complete when the auctioneer announces its completion by the fall of the hammer or in any other customary manner, and until then any bidder may retract their bid.

- The seller or his agent may set a reserve price, below which the goods will not be sold. If the seller employs a person to bid on their behalf without notifying the buyers of that right, the sale is fraudulent and voidable by the buyer.

12.8 Relevance of the Sale of Goods Act to Property Transactions

Although the Sale of Goods Act 1930 does not apply to the sale of immovable property (land and buildings), it is frequently relevant in real estate transactions in a number of practical ways:

- Sale of fixtures and fittings: When a house or apartment is sold with furniture, appliances, or fittings included in the deal, the Sale of Goods Act governs the transfer of those moveable items as part of the broader property transaction.
- Construction materials: Building materials used in the construction of a property (cement, steel, bricks, tiles) are governed by the Sale of Goods Act at the point of purchase by the developer or contractor.
- Sale of growing crops and trees: As per the definition of 'goods' in the Act, growing crops, grass, and things attached to land that are agreed to be severed before or under the contract of sale are treated as goods. For example, if a farmer sells standing crops to be harvested by the buyer, the Sale of Goods Act applies.
- Disputes over goods supplied: In cases where a builder or housing society purchases goods (such as lifts, generators, or water pumps) for a

residential property, the Sale of Goods Act governs the warranty, quality, and fitness for purpose of those goods.

Understanding the Sale of Goods Act 1930 is therefore a useful complement to knowledge of the Transfer of Property Act 1882 for anyone involved in property-related transactions in India.

Chapter 13: Law on Easements

In this chapter, we discuss what are easements and what is the the Indian law on easements.

13.1 What is easement

Easements refer to partial rights of a neighbor on another's property, other than ownership. It is the right to temporarily enter and use the neighbor's property without possessing it. They are usually linked to the enjoyment of a different neighboring property, as in the rights of easement will enable the owner of the other property to fully enjoy the property.

Examples of easements include rights of way, or right to transfer essential resources such as water or fuel, through another's private property.

Easements are of two types:

- Positive easement refers to allowing to use another's property. Examples include giving another the rights of way through one's property.

- Negative easement refers to restrictions or restraints upon the owner of the property to certain aspects of using the property, so that the other party does not face difficulty. Examples include right to access water or sunlight.

13.2 What is the Indian law on easements

The Indian Easements Act 1882 consolidates the Indian law on easements.

> THE INDIAN EASEMENTS ACT, 1882
> ACT NO. 5 OF 1882[1]
> [17th February, 1882.]
>
> An Act to define and amend the law relating to Easements and Licenses.
>
> **Preamble.**—WHEREAS it is expedient to define and amend the law relating to Easements and Licenses; It is hereby enacted as follows:—
>
> PRELIMINARY
>
> **1. Short title.**—This Act may be called the Indian Easements Act, 1882.
>
> **Local extent.**—It extends[2] to the territories respectively administered by the Governor of Madras in Council and the Chief Commissioners of the Central Provinces and Coorg:
>
> **Commencement.**—and it shall come into force on the first day of July, 1882.
>
> **2. Savings.**—Nothing herein contained shall be deemed to affect any law not hereby expressly repealed; or to derogate from—
>
> (a) any right of the [Government] to regulate the collection, retention and distribution of the water of rivers and streams flowing in natural channels, and of natural lakes and ponds, or of the water flowing, collected, retained or distributed in or by any channel or other work constructed at the public expense for irrigation;
>
> (b) any customary or other right (not being a license) in or over immovable property which the Government, the public or any person may possess irrespective of other immovable property; or
>
> (c) any right acquired, or arising out of a relation created, before this Act comes into force.
>
> [3. **Construction of certain references to Act 15 of 1877 and Act 9 of 1871.**—All references in any Act or Regulation to sections 26 and 27 of the Indian Limitation Act, 1877[5] or to sections 27 and 28 of Act No. 9 of 1871[6] shall, in the territories to which this Act extends, be read as made to sections 15 and 16 of this Act.]

Figure: First page of the Indian Easements Act 1882

The act defines what is an easement, how they are acquired and by whom they can be imposed, how the easement rights can become extinct or revoked and how they can be revived.

The act also covers temporary licenses given by one party to another, allowing them to perform certain actions related to using a property.

As per the act, definition of easement is as follows: *An easement is a right which the owner or occupier of certain land possesses, as such, for the beneficial enjoyment of that land, to do and continue to do something, or to prevent and continue to prevent something being done, in or upon, or in respect of, certain other land not his own.*

Easements can be continuous or discontinuous, or only valid for a limited time or upon certain conditions being fulfilled. Easements may be imposed, transferred or mortgaged.

Examples of easements as per the law include the following:

- *A, as the owner of a certain house, has a right of way either over his neighbour B's land for purposes connected with the beneficial enjoyment of the house. This is an easement.*

- *A, as the owner of a certain house, has the right to go on his neighbour B's land, and to take water for the purposes of his household out of a spring therein. This is an easement.*

- *A, as the owner of a certain house, has the right to conduct water from B's stream to supply the fountains in the garden attached to the house. This is an easement.*

- *A has, in respect of his house, a right of way over B's land. B may grant to C, as the owner of a neighbouring farm, the right to feed his cattle on the grass growing on the way: provided that A's right of way is not thereby obstructed.*

Chapter 14: Laws Related to Cooperative Housing Societies

In this chapter, we explore the laws, functioning, and relevance of cooperative housing societies in India. With urbanisation increasing rapidly, especially in metro cities, cooperative housing societies have become a common form of residential property ownership and management. Understanding the legal aspects of these societies is important for homeowners, prospective buyers, and tenants alike.

14.1 What is a Cooperative Housing Society?

A cooperative housing society is a legally formed body of residents who come together to manage the affairs of a residential building or housing complex. It is registered under the respective state's Cooperative Societies Act and functions on principles of cooperation, mutual benefit, and democratic decision-making. Every member of the society typically owns or occupies a flat or unit in the building and holds a share in the society.

The main purpose of such societies is to take collective responsibility for the maintenance, repairs, management, and administration of the property. They also play a key role in ensuring transparency in ownership transfers, managing common resources like water and electricity, enforcing building rules, and resolving disputes among residents.

14.2 Legal Framework Governing Cooperative Housing Societies

Housing societies in India are governed by state-specific cooperative laws. Some of the important ones include:

- The Maharashtra Cooperative Societies Act, 1960
- Delhi Cooperative Societies Act, 2003
- Karnataka Cooperative Societies Act, 1959
- Tamil Nadu Cooperative Societies Act, 1983

Each state has its own Registrar of Cooperative Societies, under whom all such societies must register and function. These laws outline rules regarding registration, bye-laws, elections, meetings, maintenance charges, dispute resolution, and dissolution of the society.

14.3 Structure and Formation of a Housing Society

To register a cooperative housing society, the following steps are generally involved:

1. A minimum number of residents (usually 10 or more) who are owners of flats in the building must come together to form the society.

2. An application is made to the Registrar along with a copy of the proposed bye-laws, list of members, affidavits, resolutions, and other documents.

3. Upon verification, the Registrar issues a certificate of registration, after which the society becomes a legal entity.

Each society is governed by its own bye-laws, which must be consistent with the state cooperative act. The bye-laws define the responsibilities of the members, managing committee, maintenance charges, quorum for meetings, and more.

14.4 Rights and Duties of Members

Rights of members include:
- Right to vote in elections of the managing committee
- Right to receive fair notice of general body meetings
- Right to inspect books of accounts and records
- Right to sell or transfer their property (subject to the society's approval process)

Duties of members include:
- Timely payment of maintenance and other dues
- Abiding by the society's bye-laws and resolutions
- Not carrying out unauthorised construction or usage of flats
- Cooperating in the peaceful running of the society

14.5 Powers and Functions of the Managing Committee

The day-to-day affairs of the society are managed by an elected Managing Committee, which includes the President, Secretary, Treasurer, and other members. Their responsibilities include:

- Calling Annual General Meetings and Special General Meetings
- Maintaining accounts and records of the society
- Managing repairs, maintenance, and utilities
- Dealing with complaints and resolving member disputes
- Ensuring compliance with bye-laws and state law

The committee is elected through democratic elections, usually every 3 or 5 years, as per the state rules.

14.6 Common Legal Issues in Housing Societies

Disputes in housing societies can arise in many areas, such as:

- Maintenance dues: Some members may default in paying dues, leading to legal action by the society.
- Transfer/NOC issues: Societies sometimes delay or deny no-objection certificates (NOCs) during sale of a flat.

- Unauthorised alterations: Members may carry out illegal constructions or changes in their flats.
- Elections and misuse of power: Managing committees may face allegations of rigging elections or financial mismanagement.
- Tenant restrictions: Some societies try to illegally bar tenants or unmarried individuals.

In such cases, members can file complaints with the Registrar of Cooperative Societies or, in some instances, approach the consumer forum or civil court.

14.7 Recent Trends and Digitisation

With increasing digitisation, many housing societies now use software platforms and apps to manage communication, billing, and complaints. States like Maharashtra have also introduced online registration and complaint portals.

The Model Bye-Laws have also been updated to include provisions on digital communication, GST on maintenance charges, and greater transparency in record-keeping.

Chapter 15: Real Estate (Regulation and Development) Act, 2016 – RERA

In this chapter, we explore the Real Estate (Regulation and Development) Act, 2016, commonly known as RERA. This law has brought significant reforms to the real estate sector in India by promoting transparency, accountability, and fairness between builders and homebuyers. Since many Indians invest their life savings into buying a flat or house, understanding RERA is crucial for protecting their rights and ensuring timely delivery of their homes.

15.1 Introduction to RERA

The Real Estate (Regulation and Development) Act, 2016 was enacted by the Parliament of India to regulate the real estate sector and address the long-standing issues of project delays, poor construction quality, and fraudulent practices by developers.

The act aims to:

- Protect the interests of homebuyers
- Boost investor confidence
- Ensure timely delivery of projects
- Increase transparency in transactions

RERA is a central law, but each state and union territory is required to establish its own Real Estate Regulatory

Authority and a Real Estate Appellate Tribunal to hear appeals.

15.2 Applicability of RERA

RERA applies to:
- All residential and commercial real estate projects where land is over 500 square meters or has more than 8 units
- Real estate agents and brokers involved in selling such properties
- All states and union territories of India, each with its own RERA website

Projects started after 1st May 2017 (or not completed by then) must register under RERA before any sale.

15.3 Key Provisions of the Act

Some of the most important provisions under RERA are as follows:

Project registration:
- All eligible real estate projects must be registered with the respective State RERA.
- The promoter must provide detailed disclosures about the project: layout plans, timeline, government approvals, financials, etc.
- A registration number is issued, which must be mentioned in all advertisements.

Separate escrow account:
- Developers are required to deposit 70% of the amount collected from buyers into a dedicated bank account.
- This amount must be used only for construction and land cost of that specific project.
- This helps prevent diversion of funds to other projects.

Advance payment restriction:
- Builders cannot accept more than 10% of the sale value as advance or booking amount without entering into a formal agreement for sale.

Timely delivery and penalty:
- Promoters are bound to complete projects as per the registered timeline.
- If delayed, the buyer is entitled to compensation, refund, or interest payment.

Structural defect liability:
- Developers must fix any structural defects or poor workmanship that arise within five years of possession, without charge.

Consent for changes:
- Any major alteration in project plans requires the consent of at least two-thirds of allottees.

Agent registration:
- Real estate agents must register under RERA and are assigned a unique registration number.

15.4 Rights of Homebuyers under RERA

RERA significantly strengthens the position of the homebuyer. Key rights include:

- Right to obtain complete project information from the builder
- Right to refund or compensation in case of delays or default
- Right to timely possession as per agreement
- Right to access documents and legal titles
- Right to file a complaint against a builder or agent for non-compliance

Homebuyers can file complaints directly with the State RERA Authority or approach the Appellate Tribunal if needed.

15.5 Penalties for Non-Compliance

Introduction to Property Law in India

RERA imposes strict penalties for violations:
- Developers who fail to register a project can face penalties up to 10% of project cost, and imprisonment for continued non-compliance.
- Agents selling without registration may be fined ₹10,000 per day up to 5% of the deal value.
- False information or fraudulent practices can also attract hefty fines and legal action.

15.6 How to Use RERA Portals

Each state has its own RERA website, where buyers can:
- Check if a project is registered
- Verify project status, approvals, and timelines
- View complaints or notices issued
- File an online complaint

Examples:
- Maharashtra RERA: https://maharera.mahaonline.gov.in
- Uttar Pradesh RERA: https://www.up-rera.in
- Karnataka RERA: https://rera.karnataka.gov.in

15.7 Impact of RERA on the Real Estate Sector

RERA has introduced a culture of compliance, discipline, and consumer protection in the real estate sector. While some developers initially resisted the changes, over time the sector has adapted. Key benefits include:

- Increase in project transparency
- Improved credibility of developers
- Empowerment of homebuyers
- Legal remedy for project delays

However, implementation varies across states and buyers must remain vigilant and proactive.

Chapter 16: Land Acquisition Laws in India

In this chapter, we examine the legal framework governing land acquisition in India, which is the process by which the government forcibly acquires private land for public use, with compensation to the landowners. Understanding land acquisition laws is crucial not just for landowners and farmers, but also for developers, policymakers, and citizens affected by large infrastructure projects.

16.1 What is Land Acquisition?

Land acquisition refers to the process by which the government acquires private land for public purposes such as building roads, railways, airports, industrial corridors, housing projects, or for strategic and defence-related use.

Unlike voluntary sale between private parties, land acquisition is compulsory, although the law mandates payment of fair compensation and provision of rehabilitation and resettlement to the affected parties.

16.2 Evolution of Land Acquisition Law

Earlier, land acquisition in India was governed by the Land Acquisition Act of 1894, a colonial-era law that gave sweeping powers to the government with minimal safeguards for landowners. It often resulted in forced evictions, low compensation, and public discontent.

In response to growing protests, social movements, and Supreme Court interventions, the old law was repealed and replaced with a new framework:

The Right to Fair Compensation and Transparency in Land Acquisition, Rehabilitation and Resettlement Act, 2013 (also called LARR Act 2013 or New Land Acquisition Act).

This act aims to balance the needs of development with the rights and dignity of affected landowners and communities.

16.3 Objectives of the LARR Act 2013

The key objectives of the new law include:
- Ensuring fair and adequate compensation to landowners
- Providing rehabilitation and resettlement (R&R) to displaced persons
- Increasing transparency and accountability in acquisition processes
- Protecting the interests of vulnerable sections like tribals and farmers
- Introducing social impact assessments before any acquisition

16.4 Applicability and Scope

The LARR Act applies to:

- All land acquisitions by the government for public purposes
- Acquisitions by private companies when land is acquired with government involvement
- Acquisitions for PPP (Public-Private Partnership) projects

However, the act does not apply to acquisitions under certain special laws like the SEZ Act, Metro Rail Acts, or national highways, unless those laws are amended.

Some states have passed their own versions or amendments to the central law, especially after the 2015 ordinances attempted to dilute some of its provisions.

16.5 Key Provisions of the LARR Act

Consent of affected people:

- For private projects, consent of 80% of affected landowners is required.
- For PPP projects, consent of 70% is required.
- No consent is needed for government projects of national importance (e.g., defence, railways).

Social Impact Assessment (SIA):

- A mandatory Social Impact Assessment study must be conducted before land is acquired.
- The study evaluates how the acquisition will affect local communities, environment, livelihoods, and displacement.
- Public hearings and expert reviews are part of the process.

Compensation:
- Compensation must be at least:
    - 2 times the market value in urban areas
    - 4 times the market value in rural areas
- Additional solatium of 100% of the compensation is awarded as a measure of goodwill.
- The market value is determined by the circle rate, sale deeds, and consent awards.

Rehabilitation and Resettlement (R&R):
R&R is mandatory in addition to compensation. It includes:
- Alternate housing and land for landless displaced families
- Employment or annuity
- Transportation and relocation allowances
- One-time grant for construction

- Skill training for alternative livelihoods

Return of unutilized land:

If acquired land remains unutilised for five years, it must be returned to the original owners or land bank of the state.

Bar on acquisition of multi-crop land:

The act discourages acquisition of multi-crop irrigated land. Such acquisition is allowed only under exceptional circumstances, and equivalent wasteland must be developed elsewhere.

16.6 Rights of Affected Persons

Under the LARR Act, affected individuals and families have the following rights:

- Right to object to the acquisition and participate in public hearings
- Right to receive notice and explanation for acquisition
- Right to challenge the acquisition in court
- Right to fair compensation and R&R benefits
- Right to be treated with dignity and humane rehabilitation

16.7 Grievance Redressal and Legal Remedies

Any aggrieved person can:

- File objections during the public consultation process
- Approach the Land Acquisition, Rehabilitation and Resettlement Authority established under the Act
- Challenge the acquisition or compensation in civil courts or High Court as per legal procedure

16.8 Challenges in Implementation

Despite progressive provisions, there have been practical issues:

- Delays in compensation and R&R
- Disputes over valuation of land
- Dilution of protections by some states
- Weak enforcement of social impact assessments
- Landowners not being properly informed of their rights

Hence, active public participation and legal awareness are essential to ensure that the spirit of the law is upheld.

Chapter 17: Benami Transactions and Benami Property Law

In this chapter, we examine the legal concept of benami property and the laws that prohibit benami transactions in India. Benami transactions have long been a source of corruption, black money, and legal complications in property ownership. The government has made efforts to curb this through stringent laws and enforcement mechanisms.

17.1 What is a Benami Property?

The term benami comes from Persian and literally means "without name." A benami transaction is one where a property is purchased by one person, but the title is held in the name of another person who is not the real owner.

The actual payer of the money is someone else, while the person in whose name the property stands is either unaware, complicit, or has no beneficial interest. The motive is often to hide illicit wealth, evade taxes, or keep assets beyond the reach of creditors or the authorities.

17.2 Legal Framework: The Prohibition of Benami Property Transactions Act, 1988

To curb such transactions, the Benami Transactions (Prohibition) Act, 1988 was passed. This was later amended and renamed as:

The Prohibition of Benami Property Transactions Act, 1988 (as amended in 2016)

The amended law came into effect on 1st November 2016, giving wide powers to the government to confiscate benami properties and punish offenders.

17.3 Definition of a Benami Transaction

According to the Act, a benami transaction is:

- A transaction or arrangement where property is transferred to or held by one person, but the consideration is paid by another person;
- And the property is held for the benefit of the person who paid for it.

The law excludes certain genuine cases, such as:

- Property held in the name of spouse or children, and paid for out of known sources;
- Property held in a HUF (Hindu Undivided Family) in the name of a member;
- Property held by a trustee or on behalf of another person in fiduciary capacity.

17.4 Examples of Benami Transactions

- Mr. A buys a house in the name of his driver, Mr. B, but pays the money himself and retains all control — this is benami.
- Ms. X buys a plot of land in the name of her aunt to avoid detection of black money — this is also benami.
- However, if Mr. Y buys a house in the name of his wife and the money comes from declared income, it is not benami.

17.5 Powers under the Benami Act

The amended Act of 2016 has established a detailed procedure and enforcement mechanism:

- Initiating Officer: Can provisionally attach a suspected benami property.
- Approving Authority: Confirms or rejects the attachment after inquiry.
- Adjudicating Authority: Determines whether the property is indeed benami.
- Appellate Tribunal: Hears appeals against orders of the Adjudicating Authority.
- Further appeal can be made to the High Court.

If a property is confirmed to be benami:

- It can be confiscated by the central government without any compensation.
- The transaction is declared null and void.

17.6 Punishment for Benami Transactions

The Act provides for strict punishment:

- Imprisonment for a term ranging from 1 year to 7 years;
- Fine up to 25% of the fair market value of the benami property;
- Persons providing false information may be punished with imprisonment up to 5 years and fine up to 10% of the property's value.

17.7 Effects and Implications for Property Owners

Property owners must take precautions to ensure:

- They have a clear title and legitimate source of funds;
- All transactions are properly documented;
- They are not holding property on behalf of others without a valid legal reason.

For buyers, it's important to check the background of the seller, source of funds, and ensure the sale is not part of a benami transaction, especially in secondary sales.

Banks and financial institutions now conduct greater due diligence while financing property purchases to ensure compliance.

17.8 Common Misconceptions

- Merely buying property in a relative's name is not automatically benami — it depends on source of funds and intention.
- Not all gifts of property are benami — if gift tax and declaration requirements are met, it may be legitimate.
- Property in the name of business partners or nominees can also fall under scrutiny if beneficial ownership is hidden.

Chapter 18: Partition and Joint Ownership of Property

In this chapter, we explore the legal aspects of joint ownership and partition of property in India. These are important issues that frequently arise in family disputes, especially in cases involving inherited property, ancestral land, or co-purchased flats. Understanding the rights of co-owners and how property can be partitioned legally is essential to avoid and resolve conflicts.

18.1 What is Joint Ownership of Property?

Joint ownership refers to a situation where two or more persons own a property together, each having a share in it. Joint ownership can arise in several ways:

- By inheritance from a common ancestor
- Through purchase in the name of multiple persons
- As part of marital or family arrangements

Each joint owner has an undivided share in the whole property, even if their names are not mentioned equally on the property documents. No co-owner can claim a specific physical part of the property unless it is partitioned.

18.2 Types of Joint Ownership

There are two main legal types of joint ownership in India:

Joint Tenancy (rare in India):
- All co-owners have equal interest
- There is a right of survivorship—upon death of one co-owner, their share passes to the others
- This form is more common in countries like the UK or USA

Tenancy-in-Common (common in India):
- Each co-owner holds a defined share, which can be equal or unequal
- There is no right of survivorship—upon death, the deceased's share passes to their legal heirs
- Common in cases of inheritance or co-purchase

18.3 What is Partition of Property?

Partition means dividing jointly owned property so that each co-owner gets a separate, identifiable share, and becomes the full owner of their portion.

Partition can be:
- By mutual agreement between co-owners
- Through a registered partition deed
- By filing a suit in civil court if no agreement is possible

Partition applies to both movable and immovable property, but is most commonly used in the context of land, houses, or flats.

18.4 How Partition is Done Legally

There are several ways to partition a property legally:

Partition by mutual agreement:
- Co-owners mutually agree on division of property
- A Partition Deed is prepared and registered
- Boundaries and shares are clearly demarcated
- Stamp duty and registration charges are applicable

Partition through family settlement:
- A family settlement agreement may be used to divide property without litigation
- It should be signed by all parties and preferably registered
- Useful in preventing future disputes

Partition by filing a civil suit:
- If co-owners cannot agree, any one of them can file a suit for partition in the civil court

- Court appoints a commissioner to survey and divide the property
- If division is not practical, court may order auction or sale and distribute the proceeds

18.5 Partition of Ancestral Property in Hindu Law

In Hindu families, ancestral property is property inherited up to four generations without any break in succession. As per the Hindu Succession Act, every coparcener (a male or female descendant up to four generations) has a birthright in ancestral property.

Any coparcener can demand partition at any time. After the 2005 amendment, daughters also have equal rights as sons in ancestral property, provided the property is not already partitioned.

Upon partition, each coparcener receives a separate share, and becomes the absolute owner of that share.

18.6 Partition among Muslim and Christian Families

Muslim Law:
- There is no concept of coparcenary in Muslim law
- Property is divided as per Islamic inheritance rules upon the death of a person

- Partition usually takes place after death and is governed by personal law, not by a right to demand partition during the owner's lifetime

Christian Law:
- Partition of property is governed by the Indian Succession Act, 1925
- All legal heirs inherit property as tenants-in-common
- Property can be partitioned either by agreement or by court

18.7 Challenges in Partition Cases

Partition often leads to disputes over:
- Unequal shares or improvements made by one party
- Possession or access to common areas like entrances or parking
- Delay in agreeing to partition or lack of cooperation
- Cases where one co-owner has died and the legal heirs must be included

In such cases, court intervention becomes necessary, and the process may take time.

18.8 Rights of Co-Owners Before Partition

Until partition is completed:

- Each co-owner has the right to reside in the whole property
- They have the right to use and enjoy the property, but not to exclude others
- They cannot sell or mortgage the entire property, but may sell their own share
- All co-owners are responsible for maintenance, taxes, and other dues proportionally

Chapter 19: Property Taxation and Municipal Duties

In this chapter, we examine the topic of property taxation and related municipal duties in India. Understanding these civic obligations is essential for any property owner, whether it is a house, flat, plot of land, or commercial premises. Property taxes are a major source of revenue for local authorities and help fund public services such as roads, sanitation, lighting, water supply, and parks.

19.1 What is Property Tax?

Property tax is a tax levied by the municipal corporation or local body on real estate. It is an annual or semi-annual tax based on the assessed value of the property, and it must be paid by the property owner.

The tax is applicable to:
- Residential homes and apartments
- Commercial buildings
- Vacant land (in some areas)
- Industrial properties

Every municipal corporation, municipality, or panchayat has its own property tax rules, rate slabs, and collection procedures.

19.2 Who Levies Property Tax?

Property tax is levied and collected by the:

- Municipal Corporation (in larger cities like Delhi, Mumbai, Bangalore, etc.)
- Municipality or Nagar Palika (in towns)
- Panchayats or Gram Panchayats (in rural areas)

These bodies function under state government laws such as:

- The Delhi Municipal Corporation Act
- The Maharashtra Municipal Corporations Act
- The Tamil Nadu Panchayats Act, etc.

Each urban local body (ULB) decides the tax rates and valuation method within the limits allowed by the state.

19.3 How Property Tax is Calculated

The property tax is typically calculated based on:

Annual Value or Unit Area Value of the property × Tax rate set by the municipality

There are three main systems used:

Annual Rental Value System (ARV):

- Based on the estimated rental value of the property, even if it is self-occupied.

Introduction to Property Law in India

- Used in older systems like in Hyderabad and Chennai.

Capital Value System (CVS):
- Based on the market value of the property as fixed by the local authority.
- Followed in cities like Mumbai.

Unit Area Value System (UAV):
- Based on the per square foot area value assigned to the location and usage type.
- Used in Bangalore and Delhi.

Example:
If a flat has a unit area value of ₹20/sq ft/month and measures 1,000 sq ft:
Annual Value = 20 × 1,000 × 12 = ₹2,40,000
If the tax rate is 10%, tax = ₹24,000 per year

19.4 Components of Municipal Duties

In addition to property tax, owners may have to pay:
- Water tax or metered charges
- Sewerage and drainage charges
- Garbage collection fees
- Betterment charges for new infrastructure

- Vacant land tax (in some cases)
- Education cess or urban development cess in select cities

These may be billed separately or included in the property tax assessment.

19.5 When and How to Pay

Most municipalities allow payment:
- Online through the corporation's website or apps
- At designated counters in municipal offices
- Via banks partnered with the municipal authority

Penalties may apply for late payment, including:
- Interest on unpaid amounts
- Fines
- In extreme cases, the property can be attached or auctioned

Some cities offer rebates for early payment or for senior citizens, women, and ex-servicemen.

19.6 Consequences of Non-Payment

If a property owner fails to pay property tax:
- The municipal body may issue a demand notice
- Interest begins accruing on the overdue amount
- Persistent non-payment can result in:

- Sealing of the property
- Disconnection of water supply
- Legal proceedings
- Auction of property to recover dues

Hence, it is important to pay taxes on time and retain the receipts for proof.

19.7 Disputes and Rectification

Sometimes property owners face issues such as:

- Wrong assessment or inflated bill
- Change in ownership not updated
- Incorrect property classification (residential vs commercial)

In such cases, the owner can file a rectification request with the Assessment Department of the municipal body, along with:

- Property documents
- Previous tax receipts
- Photographs or usage proof

Most corporations now allow online grievance redressal and tracking.

19.8 Importance of Paying Property Tax

Paying property tax on time is not only a legal obligation but also:
- Helps maintain cleaner and better infrastructure
- Keeps your ownership clear in municipal records
- Is often required for:
  - Obtaining building plan approval
  - Selling or transferring the property
  - Getting loans against property

Chapter 20: Property Disputes and Court Remedies

Property disputes are among the most common types of civil litigation in India. These disputes can involve family members, co-owners, tenants, neighbours, buyers, sellers, or even government authorities. In this chapter, we explore the nature of property disputes, their common causes, legal remedies available to aggrieved parties, and how courts handle such cases.

20.1 Nature and Types of Property Disputes

Property disputes arise when two or more parties claim conflicting rights over the same immovable property. Such disputes may relate to:

- Ownership: Who is the legal owner of a property?
- Possession: Who has the right to occupy or use the property?
- Title: Whether the title documents are valid and complete.
- Boundaries and encroachment: One party alleging trespass or illegal construction.
- Tenancy and lease: Disputes between landlords and tenants.
- Inheritance and succession: Between family members over inherited or ancestral property.

- Sale and purchase: Disputes arising from sale agreements, delayed possession, or misrepresentation.

These cases may involve private individuals, real estate developers, or government bodies, and may take years to resolve if not addressed properly.

20.2 Common Causes of Property Disputes

Some of the most frequent causes of property disputes include:

- Unclear or disputed title: Missing documents, forged papers, or incomplete registration.
- Oral family arrangements without written or registered agreements.
- Unregistered sale agreements or failure to execute a sale deed.
- Delay in mutation or transfer of property records.
- Inheritance disputes among legal heirs, especially in absence of a valid will.
- Partition disputes among co-owners or siblings.
- Encroachment or illegal occupation of land or common areas.
- Builder-buyer issues: Delay in possession, change in layout, non-delivery of promised amenities.

Understanding the root cause is important to determine the appropriate legal remedy.

20.3 Legal Forums for Property Disputes

The nature of the dispute determines which legal forum will hear the matter:

Type of Dispute	Legal Forum
Civil ownership, title, possession	Civil Court / District Court
Inheritance and succession	Civil Court / Family Court
Builder-buyer dispute	**RERA Authority** or **Consumer Forum**
Eviction or rent matters	**Rent Control Tribunal** or **Civil Court**
Government land or illegal construction	**High Court (writ petition)** or **Municipal Authorities**
Fraud or criminal encroachment	**Criminal Court** under IPC (with police complaint)

20.4 Common Legal Remedies Available

The following are key remedies that a person can seek through the courts:

Suit for Declaration (Ownership):

- Filed when a person claims legal ownership or title to a property and seeks a court declaration.
- Useful when documents are challenged or ownership is in doubt.

Suit for Injunction (To Stop Interference):
- Filed to restrain the other party from interfering with the property.
- Can be temporary (interim injunction) or permanent.
- Common in cases of trespass, illegal construction, or threats.

Suit for Possession or Eviction:
- Used to recover possession from an illegal occupant or trespasser.
- Landlords can file eviction suits against defaulting tenants.
- May be combined with damages for illegal occupation.

Suit for Partition:
- Filed when co-owners want to divide joint property.

- Court may appoint a commissioner to physically demarcate property.
- If not divisible, court may order sale and division of proceeds.

Specific Performance of Contract:
- Filed when the seller refuses to complete the sale after signing an agreement.
- Buyer can seek a court order directing completion of the sale and registration of the property.

Cancellation of Fraudulent Documents:
- If documents like sale deeds or power of attorney are forged or obtained under coercion, courts can cancel such documents.

Writ Petition in High Court:
- If government authorities are involved, one may file a writ petition under Article 226 of the Constitution.
- Useful in cases of illegal demolition, delay in registration, or unfair acquisition.

20.5 Precautions to Avoid Property Disputes

Many disputes can be prevented with the right precautions:

- Always verify the title documents before purchase.
- Conduct a title search and check for encumbrances at the Sub-Registrar's Office.
- Ensure the sale deed is registered and stamped properly.
- Pay all property taxes and dues on time.
- Get mutation done in revenue records after purchase.
- Prepare a registered will to avoid inheritance conflicts.
- Get family partitions or settlements in writing and registered.
- Use lawyers or property consultants for high-value transactions.

20.6 Delay and Cost of Litigation

Property disputes in India often drag on for years or decades due to:

- Court backlogs
- Multiple appeals
- Non-cooperation of parties
- Complex documentation and legal procedures

They also involve:

- High legal costs
- Emotional stress
- Financial lock-in of assets

As an alternative, parties may explore mediation or Lok Adalats for faster resolution.

20.7 Case Studies (Examples)

Example 1:

Mr. A inherited land from his father. His cousin B forged documents and sold it. Mr. A filed a suit for declaration and cancellation of the sale deed. The court ruled in favour of Mr. A after examining the genealogy and title records.

Example 2:

Ms. X booked a flat from a builder in 2016, but possession was delayed by 5 years. She filed a complaint under RERA and was awarded refund with interest.

Example 3:

Three brothers jointly owned ancestral property. One wanted to sell without the consent of others. A partition suit was filed, and the court ordered division through a court-appointed commissioner.

20.8 Conclusion

Property disputes are complex, emotionally charged, and legally intricate. It is advisable to:

- Maintain complete documentation
- Seek legal advice early
- Avoid verbal agreements or informal transactions
- Approach the right forum based on the nature of the issue

Being aware of one's rights and following due legal process is the best safeguard in property matters.

Chapter 21: Conclusion

In this book, we have systematically introduced and explored the multifaceted landscape of property law in India, with particular focus on how property rights are created, transferred, managed, and protected under the law. Beginning with a discussion on the fundamental concepts of property and its types, we examined the distinctions between ownership and possession—concepts at the very core of land law.

We traced the evolution of property law from ancient times through religious, philosophical, and customary traditions, highlighting influences from Roman, Islamic, and English law, as well as the unique contributions of Indian thinkers and legislators. Our historical survey showed how property law in India gradually adapted to social, economic, and technological changes, culminating in the codified statutes that shape modern practice today.

A central theme of the book has been the Transfer of Property Act, 1882, which serves as the backbone of property transactions among living persons. We delved into key modes of property transfer, including sale, mortgage, lease, exchange, and gift, explaining their essential legal requirements, the rights and liabilities of parties, and the procedural safeguards built into Indian law. The book further examined related statutes such as the Indian Succession Act, 1925, the Indian Easements Act, 1882, and the Sale of Goods Act, 1930, each contributing to the legal fabric governing property rights and succession.

We also discussed emerging trends and recent reforms: like digitalization of land records, e-registration of deeds, and the impact of landmark legislations such as the Real Estate (Regulation and Development) Act (RERA). These developments are making property transactions more transparent, efficient, and accessible to the average citizen.

Throughout, we emphasized practical aspects: the importance of clear title verification, proper documentation, and compliance with registration and stamp duty laws. We addressed the role of courts, the significance of judicial precedents, and provided guidance on remedies available in case of disputes, fraud, or breach of contract.

Property is both a fundamental human need and often the largest investment in a person's life. At the same time, it can be a major source of stress if disputes arise or if parties are unaware of their rights and obligations. For these reasons, a sound knowledge of property law is essential not only for legal professionals but for anyone who owns, intends to own, inherits, or deals with property in India.

It is hoped that this book serves as a practical and reliable guide for readers, enabling them to navigate the complex world of property law with greater clarity, awareness, and confidence.

Glossary of Legal Terms

Adverse Possession:
A legal doctrine by which a person who openly occupies land without the owner's permission, continuously and hostilely for a statutory period (usually 12 years in India), may acquire legal ownership.

Agreement to Sell:
A contract where the seller agrees to transfer property to the buyer at a future date, subject to certain terms and conditions.

Ancestral Property:
Property inherited up to four generations of male lineage, in which all coparceners have a birthright.

Assignment:
The transfer of rights or interests from one party (assignor) to another (assignee), such as the transfer of a lease.

Benami Property:
Property held in the name of one person but the actual ownership and consideration is by another, usually to conceal ownership or evade law.

Charge:
A security interest or claim over property, usually as security for a debt, but without transferring ownership or possession.

Clear Title:
A title to property that is free from encumbrances, disputes, or legal doubts, making it marketable.

Co-ownership:
A situation where two or more persons hold legal rights over the same property.

Conditional Gift:
A gift made subject to certain conditions; failure to satisfy the conditions may invalidate the gift.

Constructive Possession:
Possession where the person does not have physical custody but has the power and intention to control the property.

Deed:
A legal document that evidences the transfer, sale, gift, lease, or mortgage of property.

Encumbrance:
A claim, lien, charge, or liability attached to property that may affect its transferability, such as a mortgage or unpaid taxes.

Equitable Ownership:
An interest in property recognized by equity (justice), though not recorded in official legal title.

Exchange:
A transfer of property where ownership of one property is transferred in return for another property, not money.

Foreclosure:
A legal process by which a mortgagee (lender) obtains

ownership of the mortgaged property upon default by the mortgagor (borrower).

Gift Deed:
A legal document that records the voluntary transfer of property ownership from one person (donor) to another (donee) without any consideration.

Immovable Property:
Property that cannot be moved, such as land and buildings.

Lease:
A contractual agreement where the lessor (landlord) grants the lessee (tenant) the right to use property for a specified period in return for rent.

Legal Heir:
A person entitled by law to inherit the property of a deceased person.

Lessee:
The person to whom a property is leased (tenant).

Lessor:
The person who leases out property (landlord).

Lis Pendens:
A doctrine that prevents transfer of property under litigation until the court case is resolved.

Market Value:
The price that property would fetch in an open market between a willing buyer and seller.

Mortgage:
The transfer of an interest in specific immovable property as security for repayment of a loan or debt.

Mutation:
The process of updating land or property records to reflect a change in ownership after transfer or inheritance.

Partition:
The division of jointly-owned property into individual shares so that each co-owner gets a defined portion.

Personal Property:
Movable property that is not attached to land or buildings, such as vehicles or jewellery.

Possession:
Physical control or occupation of property, whether lawful or unlawful.

Power of Attorney (PoA):
A legal instrument by which one person authorizes another to act on their behalf in property or legal matters.

Registration:
The act of recording a property transaction in the official government records to make it legally valid.

Sale:
The transfer of ownership of property in exchange for a price paid or promised.

Stamp Duty:
A government tax paid on legal documents involved in the transfer, sale, or lease of property.

Sub-lease:
A lease granted by a lessee to another person for part or all of the leased property.

Succession:
The process by which property is passed on to legal heirs upon the death of the owner.

Tenancy-in-Common:
A form of joint ownership where each co-owner holds a specific, undivided share in the property, which can be inherited or transferred.

Title:
Legal evidence of ownership of property.

Transfer of Property:
The act by which a living person conveys property to one or more living persons.

Usufructuary Mortgage:
A type of mortgage where the lender (mortgagee) is given possession of the property and can enjoy its income until the debt is repaid.

Will:
A legal declaration by which a person names one or more persons to manage their estate and provide for the distribution of property after death.

About the Authors

Siva Prasad Bose is an author of various introductory guidebooks related to aspects of Indian laws. He is currently retired after many years of service in Uttar Pradesh Power Corporation Limited. He received his engineering degree from Jadavpur University, Kolkata and has a law degree from Meerut University, Meerut. His interests lie in the fields of family law, civil law, law of contracts, and any areas of law related to power electricity related issues.

Joy Bose is a software engineer and a data scientist by profession.

Other Books by Siva Prasad Bose

Introduction to Wills and Probate

Senior Citizens Abuse in India

Introduction to negotiable instruments

Introduction to marriage laws in India

Neighbor Problems in India and what to do about them

Managing Court Cases with Mental Strength

Delays in Court Cases in India

Introduction to Patents and Patent Law in India

www.ingramcontent.com/pod-product-compliance
Lightning Source LLC
Chambersburg PA
CBHW071502220526
45472CB00003B/893